A GUIDE
to
MASS MEDIA
in
HIGHER ENGLISH

by

Eleanor Thomson, B.A. (Hons.),
Dip. Ed., M. Litt.

ISBN 0 7169 3159 1
© E. Thomson, 1991.

ROBERT GIBSON · Publisher
17 Fitzroy Place, Glasgow, G3 7SF.

INTRODUCTION

This guide is intended for the candidate who has little or no knowledge of the Mass Media and who is preparing for the Mass Media option in the S.C.E. Higher Grade English Examinations.

Intending candidates will find the following stylistic features of this guide useful:

1. Clear, step by step introduction to the Mass Media for S.C.E. English with a summary of the main points covered in each chapter.

2. Specialist terms for Media Studies are highlighted, providing a key to the Glossary of Terms at the end of the book.

3. Select Annotated Bibliography.

Note: Study of the mass media should not be tackled without the expert guidance of your teacher and the information contained in this book is not an alternative to, or in any way a replacement for, classroom work with teacher guidance.

Printed by Bell and Bain Ltd., Glasgow

CONTENTS

LIST OF ILLUSTRATIONS

CHAPTER ONE

STUDYING THE MEDIA

The study of *the media* is as important, today, as studying literature. The media are an important influence in the modern world. Like literature, they help to shape ideas and values in the field of culture and, indeed, of society itself but, unlike literature, the *mass media* reach a vast number of people very quickly, often instantaneously and often they are not of high quality. Furthermore, the media are becoming more and more pervasive in our society. Judging from recent developments, new job opportunities connected directly or indirectly with the media, whether in editorial, artistic or production fields, will arise in the future as mass communication will continue to grow. It makes sense, therefore, to study the mass media, both from a personal and from a vocational point of view.

Media Studies is a subject which is devoted to analysing the mass media. This means that a study is made of how the media are produced, the kinds of messages they contain and how we make sense of such messages. Some examples of mass media are television, newspapers, radio, pop music, magazines, popular fiction and films. Just as studying English involves close analysis of drama, prose and poetry, studying the mass media involves close analysis of different media forms, or *genres*.

The mass media can be defined as:

 (i)   forms of *communication* which

 (ii) reach a mass *audience* and which

 (iii) have been designed (or *constructed*) to inform and/or entertain that audience.

This way of looking at the media breaks the complex processes of mass communication into three important areas for study. These areas are discussed in more detail on the following page.

(i) The media as forms of communication

As you read this book you will learn that you already possess useful knowledge which can be used to analyse the media. For example, it could be argued that we are all quite efficient at communicating from the earliest moments of our lives; even the sound of a baby crying communicates. By crying, the baby is communicating that something is wrong. Perhaps the baby is uncomfortable, needs food, water or, simply, the loving touch of another human being. Our response to a baby's cries, (to investigate its needs), demonstrates our ability to make meaning from what we observe. Effective communication, therefore, relies on our ability to "read" and understand a whole variety of phenomena.

We have a habit of constructing, or making, meaning for ourselves from the everyday things which we come across in our society. For example, if we walk down a busy street in town, we will see people, shop windows, cars, traffic signs, and a host of other things which will be meaningful. By looking at their clothing, their age, bearing and facial expression, we can categorise people into old, young, fashionable, dowdy, kind, beautiful or ugly. By glancing at the displays in shop windows we are likely to find out what kind of products are being sold inside each shop. We can understand cars in terms of their cost and colour, make and age, possible top speeds and their fuel consumption. We will look carefully at traffic signs before we decide whether or not it is safe to cross the road. The list is endless. We "read" all these things quite automatically, rarely thinking too much about them.

To demonstrate this, I would like you to imagine a situation such as this: you are sitting in a dentist's waiting room with several other people. It is very quiet in the room but in the background you can hear the whine of the dentist's drill. There is a strong smell of antiseptic in the air and an even stronger smell of aftershave from the man sitting to your left. You notice that another man sitting opposite to you stares straight above your head, studying the travel poster advertising Switzerland which you know is pinned high up on the wall just behind your chair. The woman sitting to your right has her eyes closed. A little boy playing on the floor at his mother's feet gives you a happy smile which you acknowledge by smiling in return. His mother is sitting with her head down, reading a magazine which she has taken from

6

several other, similar, magazines lying on the coffee table in front of her. No one has spoken but communication has taken place, nevertheless.

Communication has taken place because **messages** have been conveyed on several different **channels**:

Visual channels (what you see): the man staring at the travel poster above your head, the woman with her eyes closed and the woman reading the magazine are, consciously or unconsciously, through their behaviour, communicating the fact that they do not wish to speak. It is difficult to begin a conversation with someone who appears to be asleep, or is otherwise ignoring you. The little boy has communicated by smiling at you. By smiling back at him, you have completed this communicative act. The poster communicates information about Switzerland by using images and words. The magazine which the woman is reading communicates in a similar way; the words and images in magazines are directed at particular audiences and are likely to inform and entertain.

Aural channels (what you hear): sounds such as the dentists' drill remind you of where you are. The fact that there is silence amongst people who are sitting together is also significant.

Olfactory channels (what you smell): smells, such as the man's aftershave and the antiseptic, communicate in different ways. Perfumes, like after-shave, are a method of making oneself more desirable or socially acceptable but the smell of antiseptic has different **connotations** associated with killing bacteria.

It is, therefore, possible to make meaning from all of these things because we receive information through our senses and use our previous experience to help us understand this information. This way of looking at communication is based on **semiotics** or **semiology**, which is the name given to the study of **signs**. We will return to this subject in the next chapter.

Basically, then, communication happens when a message is sent in some form

7

or other, received through one or more of our five senses, and understood by us. This can be illustrated in very simple terms:

$$SENDER \rightarrow MESSAGE \rightarrow MEDIUM \rightarrow RECEIVER$$

i.e.   (i)   The **sender** (person(s) or machine(s))

      (ii)   sends the **message** (something meaningful)

     (iii)   through a particular **channel** (medium or method used to send the message)

     (iv)   to the **receiver** (person(s) or machine(s), for processing, in order to make meaning).

There are many, more complicated, communication models which are used to describe communication but this very basic model is sufficient for our purposes.

The first thing to notice about this model of communication is that it shows communication as a "one way" process. It does not allow for "**feedback**", e.g. if this model were applied to two people holding a conversation it could be used only to show the flow of information from one of the people talking, because the arrows point from "sender" to "receiver". Any "feedback" or reply from the other person is missing from this model.

Communication by the mass media *seems* to be "one way" but if we take a closer look, we find that we, the audience, can respond to the media. We can, for example, switch our television sets off, or decide not to buy an advertised product.

Each kind of medium sends distinctive messages to the public, the "receivers". ("Media" is the plural of "medium". Television, press, film, books, videos, music, etc., are collectively known as "the media".) There are often millions of receivers, hence the name "mass" media. Each of us have different points of view, different backgrounds, different circumstances and because of this, we each respond to the media in different ways. We can see this idea working when we compare, for example, reactions to advertisements on television. Someone might say, "I hate that advertisement!", whilst someone else might say, "I think it's funny. I quite like it.", whereas another person might ask, "Which advertisement? I can't say that I've ever noticed it!"

(ii) You, the audience

The idea of "audience" is quite complex and this aspect of the media will be given more attention in the next chapter. Meantime, it is more important to understand that we are exposed to selected and constructed messages from the mass media every day of our lives. Consequently, even although we might not be aware of the fact, we are already quite expert at deciphering the meanings which are specifically found in different media. The many hours which we have already spent watching television, reading magazines, going to the cinema, listening to the radio or pop music, have nurtured in us certain expectations about the content and construction of various media.

I would like to demonstrate this. Imagine, for a moment, that you are watching a television drama. The main character is sitting quietly talking to another character. He is discussing an incident from his past. Slowly, the picture on your screen begins to fade into darkness, and, simultaneously, the sound begins to drop until his voice fades to a murmur. Almost without thinking, we would know exactly what this means and would have certain expectations about what is going to happen next. We are unlikely, for example, to think that our television set has developed a fault, or that the story has finished unless there were other indications to this effect, e.g. the screen remains blank or the *credits* come up on the screen! Instead, we would fully expect that the screen would light up again, that the sound would return, and that the next sequence of *images* which we would see on the screen would deal in some way with the man's verbal account of his past. This is an example of one of the many *technical codes* which are used in television and film in order to move from one image to another; this particular code is called a "*fade*".

So, you see, we already possess knowledge which has been gained quite naturally from watching television. Indeed, this is one of the most exciting

9

things about studying the media; the fact that you, the student, already possess a wealth of knowledge which can be drawn upon when analysing media products in the classroom.

We cannot, however, rely on this kind of "common" knowledge alone, to pass an exam. We are able to read and write but this does not make us experts in English literature. To be able to criticise English literature, it is necessary not only to appreciate the craft of writing but to have a critical language which allows us to speak about our appreciation, i.e. we should be able to recognise and discuss similes, metaphors, onomatopoeia, etc., to name just a few of the "technical terms" which we would need before we could express our views about literature in a sensible way. Similarly, to be able to criticise media products, we must possess a critical language which is suited to that purpose.

The Scottish Examination Board (S.E.B) have the following points to make about a critical language for analysing the media:

> "As with other aspects of the English course it is important that the study of the mass media should encourage discussion, reflection and the opportunity for personal responses **sustained by a register of critical language**." (My emphasis). Scottish Examination Board, *Revised Arrangements in English*, 1987, p.34.

This does not mean that you have to laboriously learn a huge list of words and their meaning. Instead, you will gradually learn these words by using them as you analyse a variety of media products with your teacher. Neither does it mean that you will have to learn a whole new set of skills. The same kind of critical skills which you have already applied to literary texts will apply when you are analysing the media.

Many of the words which are most useful when analysing media products can be found in the Glossary of Terms in this book and because you will recognise many of the ideas which the words contain, the task of adding them to your own vocabulary should not be too difficult with a little effort on your part.

(iii)   Constructing information and entertainment

The mass media are designed, or constructed, to appeal to a variety of different audiences. We tend to forget this basic fact when we read a newspaper, or listen to the radio or watch television; the "information" which we receive from the media has been selected — choices have been made for us about what is and is not entertaining or informative. A glance at the headlines of three or four different newspapers published on the same day will demonstrate this fact. (Compare the headlines in Appendix I from the front pages of the *Daily Record* and *The Glasgow Herald*.) One item of news may have been important enough to appear on the front page of all the national newspapers — perhaps a natural disaster, or the outbreak of war between two countries — but each headline will deal with the news item in a different way according to the ideas of the journalists and editors. These ideas are likely to be further modified by the amount of space available in the newspaper.

When we listen to authoritative accounts of world news on television, we forget that these news items have been chosen from the hundreds of happenings which the news broadcasters find out about every day. The other items might be ignored because they are not considered to be important enough or simply because there is no time to use the item because "The News" is alloted a limited *time slot* in a sequence of programmes.

Further selection happens when the audience decide whether or not to read, listen to, or watch these items but it must be remembered that our choices can be made only from what has already been chosen for us by those who run the media industries.

All mass media share the distinction of being manufactured for the consumption of a large number of people: this means that money, time and effort have been put into the making of the media. Like many other industries, the media have to make money in order to carry on manufacturing. We are the consumers of the media industry's output and we pay in many different ways for what we consume. We may pay licence money to the British Broadcasting Corporation or we may pay indirectly through advertising. Think, for example, about the number of advertisements which

11

appear in newspapers and in commercial radio and television. These media industries rely on the revenue gained from advertising and try to attract large audiences in order to attract advertisers. The general public have two roles to play in this: as "consumers" not only of the products from the media industries such as pop music, commercial television, commercial radio and the print industries, but of the very products which are being advertised in the "commercials" which punctuate our listening or viewing, or which appear in magazine or newspaper advertisements.

These industries, therefore, are very competitive. Even the non-commercial sectors of the media such as the B.B.C., have to compete for listeners and viewers against the commercial stations. An understanding of the media must take into account this complex interplay between the media industries and the audiences for whom they cater.

So far, we have had a brief overview of how we might approach our studies of the media. Three main ideas were selected for discussion:

(i)   The media are forms of communication which send messages.

(ii) All messages from the media are constructed, or puposely made to inform and/or entertain.

(iii) The audience is a mass audience.

Perhaps the most important idea to carry away from this chapter is the idea of CONSTRUCTION. Media messages are constructed by many people. A television play, for example, involves *scripting*, *directing* and *producing*, which can only be achieved in co-operation with an often huge number of skilled professional people who have had training in, e.g. operating lighting, cameras and sound; *editing* video to create a coherent story from hundreds of shots; acting, and the creative skill of wardrobe and makeup personnel which enhance the actor's performance. These people, and many more, all have a hand — either directly or indirectly — in creating a play which we, the audience, will be prepared to spend some time watching.

We, of course, are also making meaning from the sounds and images being broadcast to us — exactly in the way that we do when we walk down the high street, or enter the dentists' waiting room! Construction, therefore, is a very important idea and one which you should always bear in mind when examining the mass media.

Thus far, we have been exploring the definition of mass media given at the beginning of this chapter. This has helped us to understand more about what the media is and how we are involved with it but, in order to begin analysing the media properly, we have to shape some questions from that definition. For example:

1. If the media are forms of communication, who makes the messages being communicated?

2. If the media intend to reach mass audiences, who are these audiences?

3. If the media are purposely designed or constructed, why and how are they put together?

4. If I am a consumer of the media, how effective do I find these messages?

It is from these four basic questions that the following approaches to analysing the media are derived. When analysing Mass Media, we should ask:

Who constructs media messages?
Who are the intended audiences for these messages?
For what purpose are media messages constructed?
What methods are used to make these messages?
How effective are these messages?

The purpose of the following chapter is to look more closely at these important points.

Summary of the main points raised in this chapter

Media Studies is a subject which devotes itself to in-depth analysis of the media. The huge variety of different media which we see in society today are forms of communication from which we make meaning.

The mass media can be loosely defined as forms of communication which reach a mass audience and which inform or entertain that audience.

Although we have knowledge and experience of the media which can be drawn upon when analysing various media products, we must also have the critical language which will allow sensible discussion of media products.

We already possess media knowledge and critical skills gained from studying literary texts which we can utilise when analysing media products.

Media can be categorised into commercial and non-commercial concerns (concerns which are designed to make money or which are not money making).

The media are all constructed, that is, media messages are put together by many different people. We must ask ourselves the following questions when analysing media products: Who constructs media messages? Who are the intended audience for these messages? For what purpose are media messages constructed? What methods are used to make these messages? How effective are these messages?

CHAPTER TWO

LOOKING CLOSELY AT MASS MEDIA

In the previous chapter, the following questions were posed: Who constructs media messages? Who are the intended audiences for these messages? For what purpose are media messages constructed? What methods are used to make these messages? How effective are these messages? These questions are intended as general points of entry when analysing media products.

Before exploring these questions, I would like to begin by looking more closely at *semiology*, as promised in the last chapter.

(i)   A critical language

Semiology is the study of signs and contributes towards the "language" used to analyse media products. Many of the words and phrases which you will learn during your course of studies will have emerged from this discipline. You will begin to use these terms quite naturally while you are studying the media in the classroom because they will be linked to the tasks which your teacher will give you to do.

The important thing to understand about semiology is that it represents a "way of looking" at things which is, basically, quite natural to us. If you were able to understand the imaginary situation in the dentist's waiting room (see pages 6 – 8), which demonstrated that we read information into everyday situations, then you were sharing in that particular "way of looking".

This "way of looking" involves making meaning from the information we receive through our *senses*. The simplest way to explain this is to say that *semiologists* call little pieces of information "signs" from which we can make meaning. For example, during our day to day interaction, we are likely to look for *signs* such as facial expressions (smiles, grimaces, frowns) to tell us what people are thinking or feeling.

We cannot, however, decide at random that something is meaningful. Signs are combined in a meaningful way according to rules which everyone in

15

society shares. These rules form *codes*. For example, we can say that the frown belongs to codes, or sets of rules, which we recognise in connection with bodily "communication". It would be unlikely that we would say that a person is happy when we saw them frowning (unless we lived in a society where this interpretation was accepted or unless this was a peculiarity belonging to that particular person).

Everyone is quite adept at reading signs and understanding codes because these originate in the society in which we live. All of this is based, therefore, within the social structure of society, e.g. if we return to the idea of "reading" body language, we find that Americans and Europeans use a handshake to greet people whereas Lapps rub noses and Polynesians will take your hand and stroke their own face with it (*Bodily Communication* by Michael Argyle)[1]. How we make meaning from signs and codes, therefore, depends on the *conventions* of our society.

Semiology, therefore, could be said to be concerned with the following questions:

1. What are the basic units — signs — which are present in any *text*?

2. How are these put together to make meaning?

3. In what way do these meanings relate to the social structures of our society?

These questions can be used in relation to the media. When we read a sentence in a newspaper, we are *decoding* meaning; we are making meaning from small units of information, e.g. the letters, words and phrases which make sentences; the newspaper layout, e.g. the columns, bold lettering, italic lettering, the black lines which separate one article from another; the kind of words used to create tone and the many other small points from which we create meaning. Finally, all of these things can be placed against our social and cultural setting. When we make meaning in this way — by combining signs — this is called a *syntagm*.

Similarly, when we go to the cinema to watch a film, we begin decoding the messages on the screen immediately the film begins. We listen to the music and decide whether it is lively, sad or soothing. We watch the images on the screen and decide where and when the action is taking place. We make judgements about the characters in the film and we draw on our social and cultural knowledge to make meaning from all of these things.

Such "readings" will obviously vary in relation to the kinds of media being studied but many codes and conventions overlap between different media.

For example, we apply some of the basic rules to "reading" photographs as we do to "reading" moving images. The lighting in a photograph can reveal much about the subject and mood of the photograph. The lighting used in film and television will have similar meanings. Dark lighting will produce a "creepy" or gloomy mood. Bright lighting (called *high-key*) is likely to have the opposite effect. These rules are generally understood by those who construct the media and such rules are used extensively to achieve particular affects for the benefit of the audience who will view the images.

The audience will make meaning from what they read or from what they see. This happens with *narrative*, a word which should be familiar to you from use in the English classroom. The basic meaning of the word remains the same — a story — whether we are talking about a novel or a film or a television play or, indeed, about the programmes which make up a whole evening's viewing on television.

Narratives are constructed in novels by a process of linking language. Narratives are constructed in film and television by a process of linking, amongst other things, *shots*, i.e. linking different images. The differences which can be found between film and television narratives will be discussed at greater length in Chapter Five but, meantime, my aim is to demonstrate that you are already familiar with the basic methods used to construct these narrative forms and that this provides a firm basis from which to start looking at the different methods of "telling the story" in film and television.

When we study English literature, we examine the effectiveness of poetry, plays, novels and short stories by looking closely at the language used by the poets, playwrites and authors who have created these works. When we study the Mass Media, we examine the effectiveness of various media forms, or *genres*, by looking closely at images, sounds and words.

17

This has been a very brief introduction to the idea of a critical language, derived in part from semiology, which we can use to examine the effectiveness of the mass media. Hopefully, it has not frightened or confused you but has reinforced the notion that the language of criticism should be welcomed as a necessary tool with which to work and not merely dismissed in a pejorative way as "jargon" and something to be ignored. This language can only be used effectively as part of your course of work. You cannot get away with learning a few terms such as "sign" and "code" and liberally sprinkling them through your composition. You will only be able to use them in a sensible way if you attempt to understand the ideas which they express.

(ii)   Who constructs media messages?

The mass media are organised into industries and institutions. It is important, therefore, to consider the media in the light of the personnel who produce media products and the financial constraints under which they operate.

In order to understand this better, imagine that you are standing in a car showroom. You have £20,000 to spend on a car. You are walking slowly across the room looking at the cars on display. You are looking at the colours, the high shine on the paintwork, the upholstery, the amount of space for passengers, the instruments. You are absorbing an enormous amount of information about these beautiful machines and constructing your own ideas, likes and dislikes, in relation to each car.

One thing is certain, however; you are not thinking about the various stages which these cars went through as they were being built. The fact that they began their lives, like all cars on the road, as pieces of metal, various engine components, paint in liquid form, rubber and plastic, oil and bolts, means little to you. You are only interested in the finished product! This, of course, is the intention of those who made the motor cars; they have worked to make the cars as attractive as possible for you, the consumer.

Finally, we are unlikely to consider the fact that all of the component parts which made these motor cars have had to be bought by someone in the first place. We rarely think about the shareholders — the owners of car industries.

Exactly the same ideas apply to media products. Media products result from the efforts of many different people: the people who own the industries, the people who make decisions about the products of these industries and the people who produce. We rarely think about them; we are too busy reacting to each media product much in the same way as we react to other manufactured products like the cars we looked at in our showroom!

Like other forms of production, different media genres will be produced in different ways by people who are expert in different fields. (Although a sausage factory "manufactures" goods to sell to the public, it will have different manufacturing equipment to that of the car factory and will have experts who know more about sausages than cars!) The management structure of both the car and sausage factories are, however, likely to be much the same.[2]

Media products, therefore, are "constructed" just like any other product. What you see on your television screen, cinema screen, in the newspapers and in other media has been put together through the efforts of many ordinary people who have chosen to specialise in careers in the media instead of the sausage factory!

This means that the people who work in these industries must take into consideration the amount of money available to produce the finished product, and the wishes of all the people involved in making the product, e.g. the amount of money available to a film *producer* will determine how elaborate the film will be, or how many *stars* can feature in his film (if any).

(iii) Rules and conventions of construction

Because it is likely that most of these people will be experienced in making films, they will know the rules and conventions which already exist in relation to films and film making and even although they may consciously decide to break some of these rules, they are still working within a certain set of parameters.

For example, you are likely to hear about the creative individuality of certain people in the media: certain film producers leave a stamp of individuality on

19

their films (Hitchcock, for example) or certain actors lend special significance to the part they play (John Wayne, for example) but these people are still aware of the rules which control film making or acting and their individuality is best seen against the background of "normal" methodology practised by others in the profession.

A good parallel when thinking about rules and conventions in the media, is to think about the rules and conventions which we follow when reading and writing. Before we can write, we must learn what each letter of the alphabet means. We must then learn to put the letters together into a meaningful whole in order to form words and then sentences. Listening to young children talking, we can laugh at some of their expressions: "flied" instead of "flew", for example, or "drinked" instead of "drank". These absurdities of expression arise because the children have learned that in many cases, the past tense of a verb is expressed by adding the suffix "ed" and they apply this rule indiscriminately until they learn that, conventionally, there are words which we use instead of these suffixes.

A comparison of extracts from two poems allows us to see how two poets have followed the rules and conventions of poetry but in the process, have produced two totally different points of view from the same subject. Ted Hughes writes about a hawk in *Hawk Roosting*. George Mackay Brown also writes about a hawk in his poem, *The Hawk*. If we look at the points of view of each poet, we find that in *Hawk Roosting*, Hughes *is* the hawk, whereas in *The Hawk*, George Mackay Brown is narrating the moments in a hawk's life over a week, and its eventual death at the hands of a crofter who shoots it.

Hawk Roosting

I sit in the top of the wood, my eyes closed.
Inaction, no falsifying dream
Between my hooked head and hooked feet:
Or in a sleep rehearse perfect kills and eat.

The Hawk

On Sunday the hawk fell on Bigging
and a chicken screamed
Lost in its own little snowstorm.
And on Monday he fell on the moor
And the Field Club
Raised a hundred silent prisms.

20

As you can see from these extracts, both poets have treated their subject in totally opposite ways; using different points of view and different verse structures within the same genre — poetry. These poems, of course, have been written by one person in each case — the poet. In television, film and other media genres, the end product is the result of the efforts of many people. Nevertheless, the parallels can be understood; rules and conventions always exist but they can be endlessly varied in order to produce something distinct and unique.

You might like to try this simple exercise to help you find out about the number and variety of personnel involved in making media products: the next time you are watching television, take a pencil and paper and make a note of the various people who have helped to make the programme you have just watched. Their names and job titles will appear at the end of the programme. You could also carry out the same exercise for any film you watch. Try to find out as much as you can about their jobs.

(iv)   Who are the intended audiences for these messages?

The straightforward answer to the above question is: you and I, the media consumers. With this simple fact, however, comes a complexity of ideas; we must take into consideration the idea of our individual tastes, accessibility to the media, and understanding of media products. My taste in music is likely to differ from yours. You may have a **satellite dish** which allows you to receive programmes on your television which I do not have access to because I do not have a satellite dish. We might take different meanings from a television programme because we come from different backgrounds, have been educated in a different way and have had different experiences of the world.

The word "audience" is deceiving, therefore. We tend to think of a homogeneous group of people who are confined together, watching or listening to the same things which makes us think of audiences as being passive in nature. We are not passive receivers, as I have already discussed. We make meaning from the constructed messages we see on television, or on the cinema screen or in magazine advertisements. In order to make meaning we draw on our **social and cultural knowledge**. This, in turn, will vary in relation to the **age**, **gender**, and **social and economic background** of each individual.

21

Audiences, therefore, are complex in nature: all the more so when we consider the huge range of people which the mass media must cater for.

Various media organisations such as press and magazine industries, radio and television, and the advertising industry produce at regular intervals information about audiences. Surveys are made amongst the public to find out who watches, listens, reads and buys what. Organisations such as the Broadcasters' Audiences Research Board (BARB) or Independent Local Radio (ILR) produce information on the basis of sample audiences. The BARB relies on information from meters which have been placed in the television sets of viewers to tell them which programmes are watched and the ILR ask listeners to keep diaries of what they listen to.

In advertising it is important to know about consumers. The spending power of audiences is obviously the most important consideration when the main aim of an advertisement is to persuade someone to part with money. Audiences, therefore, are graded according to the amount of money they are likely to have. These grades are shown in Figure 1.

Figure 1 — Classification of Social Grades

	Social Status	Occupation
A	Upper Middle Class	higher managerial, administrative or professional
B	Middle Class	intermediate managerial, administrative or professional
C_1	Lower Middle Class	supervisory or clerical and junior
C_2	Skilled Working Class	skilled manual
D	Working Class	semi- and unskilled manual workers
E	Those of Lowest Level of Subsistance	state pensioners or widows, casual, lowest-grade workers.

(Classification of Social Grades according to the National Readership Survey)

The media, in catering for a "mass" audience will generally attempt to fashion their end products — television programmes, advertisements, newspapers or magazines — to attract as many people as possible within the categories of age, gender and economic and social backgrounds. In this way, "markets" are created by the advertising industry and "audiences" are created by film, television, radio, press and magazine industries simply because their products are then constructed to satisfy the needs of people in these different categories. For example, I may not enjoy the currently popular Australian Soap Opera, *Neighbours*, whereas just about every child and teenager whom I know does!

The British Soap Opera, *East Enders*, is a popular programme but I wonder if you know that it was the result of a great deal of market research amongst the public? If you watch it regularly you will note that there is a fair cross-section of the average population amongst the characters: elderly, middle-aged, young, teenage, babies/children, most of whom are likely to suffer the usual problems and crises which the average individuals who form an audience will encounter during a lifetime such as marriage, divorce, illness, death, professional and personal success or failure, happiness, misery and so on.

Even although the media often make contact with their audiences (by using surveys, meters, diaries, questionnaires) we must accept that the audience — although having power to switch off their television sets or change channels; to buy or not buy a newspaper or magazine; to go or not go to the cinema, cannot easily exert a *direct* influence on the media.

Because the media categorise audiences in a way which creates neat divisions between the masses, this means that the media "speak" to us in ways which are decided according to which audience is being addressed. If we take a close look at television presenters, the people employed to talk to mass audiences, we can see clearly how this operates. Jane Root in *Open the Box*,[3] a book about television, tells us that:

> "Presenters come in many styles: like dog owners at Crufts we are adept at recognising the different breeds. We can distinguish the collar and tie-d seriousness of newsreaders from the dungareed idiocy of the hosts on children's programmes and pop shows. We realise 'gurus' like David Attenborough and Jonathan Miller will offer a very different style of programme from 'men of the people' like Terry Wogan." (page 52)

If we take the idea of catering for certain audiences further, we can see that this might bring about certain phenomena. We might ask ourselves if we, as an audience, are sometimes made **stereotypical** by the media, e.g. if you care to look closely at the kind of magazines produced for the young female teenage market, containing picture stories, you will see that most of these stories are set either in school or at home or indoors where the main characters are seen sitting or standing in pairs or groups, talking to each other (which suggests that girls are rarely active, outdoor types). The stories are likely to revolve around a character's infatuation for a particular boy in her class or school and to contain scenes of jealousy between the teenage girl characters (which suggests that all teenage girls are preoccupied only with boys and that they are constantly extremely catty to each other).

Sometimes, therefore, in order to communicate with us the mass media takes only some of the truth and leaves out many other truths. The **images** which are created of us — the audience — is sometimes distorted. It is useful, therefore, to give some thought to how it seems the media see us — their audience — by closely analysing what the media produce for our consumption.

Jean-Luc Godard, a very famous film producer, once said that "Television doesn't make Programmes — it makes viewers." Taking into account what you have understood from reading this study guide, so far, compile an outline for a composition supporting that statement using media which you yourself have experienced to illustrate your point of view.

(v)   For what purpose are media messages constructed?

If we return to the definition of mass media given earlier, in Chapter One:

  (i) forms of communication which

 (ii) reach a mass audience and which

(iii) have been designed (or constructed) to inform and/or entertain that audience,

we can see that the third section in this definition mentions two separate purposes for communicating: to *inform* and/or *entertain* an audience.

The mass media is an important source of information about our world. Newspapers, television and radio supply us with up-to-the-minute information about local, national and international affairs. Technology such as orbiting satellites which are capable of relaying signals back to earth, fibre optic cables, fax machines and computerised type-setting have increased the rate at which news can be gathered and printed or **broadcast** to audiences throughout the world.

The mass media entertains millions of people. We are entertained by television and cinematic films; videos; television and radio coverage of sport; soap operas, plays, comedy, game shows on television; audio recordings of music; books, magazines and newspapers.

Because the media are so widespread and available to many people, it has also been said that they are capable of persuading individuals to buy a product, or to believe that certain groups or nations behave in a particular way, or that people can even be persuaded to vote in a particular way. There are many arguments about these points and much research has been carried out in an attempt to find out whether or not the media have an effect on, e.g. young people, perhaps making them more violent through watching "video nasties" or violent films in the cinema.

Whether or not these things do happen, and the behaviour of individuals in audiences is directly affected by what they see is academic, needing much more discussion than we have room for here. What is more important to bear in mind for our own media analyses, is the fact that media messages are constructed for specific audiences and are intended to have an impact on that audience.

Advertisements are intended to inform the public about a particular product in the hope that they will buy it. Imagine that you have recently invented a new product — a hover-board — which skims along the ground faster than a skate-board because it is frictionless. You want to advertise this wonderful new invention.

This can be done in a simple way by merely printing a few facts about the products on a leaflet and hand-delivering these in the neighbourhood. Would

25

you, however, be reaching the correct "audience" for your product? Who, therefore, should be your "target" audience: young people or old people? How would you ensure that your leaflet is not simply thrown away? Would you make it colourful? Or would you offer money off, or some other benefit, if the client produces the leaflet when purchasing your product?

Advertisements produced by the advertising industry are constructed with similar thoughts to these in mind. They are aimed at particular audiences and are designed to make the product seem very attractive in order that the target audience will be tempted into buying it. Advertisements are, therefore, intended to be persuasive.

Other media target their audience, too, in order to inform or entertain their audience. The media produce what they believe their audiences will watch, listen to or read.

Sometimes it is easy to categorise media products as either "entertainment" or "information" but there are many different kinds of media which combine the two concepts. Try to categorise everything you watch on television under the two headings:

1. Information
2. Entertainment.

A question which you might like to give some thought to is: can we simply categorise media in this way? Are some media constructs both informative *and* entertaining? (e.g. some television advertisements.)

(vi)   What methods are used to make these messages?

The methods used to construct media products will, of course, vary in relation to different media and will be closely aligned to the question of who produces the media. For example, newspaper production requires experts in journalism as well as experts in the technology which produces the actual physical end product — the newspaper. Each newspaper is carefully planned and contains news which has been gathered and selected before being printed and distributed to its readers.

By investigating the methodology behind production processes, we can begin to understand why media products take a specific form or have a specific content.

Unfortunately, to discuss all of the methodologies for all of the media, here, would take more space than I have available. By looking briefly at one medium, however, we might grasp the intention behind asking questions about methodology.

Newspaper production has changed radically over the past few years. Methods of production using new technology such as computers and speedier methods of communication bring our newspapers to the news-stand faster than ever before. This is interesting in itself because it makes the news we read more up-to-the-minute and colourful, with new technology which allows colour processing, but by looking even more closely at newspapers and their production methods, we will see that production methods can affect the news we read.

The amount of physical space available in a newspaper can restrict the amount of information which we read. If there are two important stories, the editor must decide which story will make the headlines. Similar choices are made when sub-editors are trimming news stories to fit the space available on a newspaper page. Ask yourself if you really are seeing the true story the next time you look at a newspaper photograph. Pictures in newspapers are often trimmed to fit the space available on the front page.

These constraints caused by the practicalities of production are a good reason for studying production methods. The world which we are shown by the media is a constructed world; a world which has been interfered with during the process of production. The world which we see on the television screen, therefore, or read about in the newspapers, or watch on the big screen in the cinemas is mediated to us: choices have been made during production and these choices often mean that the mediated words and images which we take for granted as a reflection of "reality" are, in fact, processed and, therefore, altered versions of reality. By understanding how media production processes work, we might be in a better position to understand that the media does not supply the public with the "truth" but only partial truths; constructs of reality which, because of limitations of space, time or other such practicalities, cannot include everything.

We tend to grade the media into what is "informative" and, therefore, "truthful" and what is "entertaining" and, therefore, mimetic or "untruthful" rather in the same way that we would categorise a biography as "fact" and, therefore, something which is "truthful", and an adventure story as "fiction" and, therefore, something which is "untruthful".

Newspapers, the news on television, documentaries, etc., are expected to "tell us the truth" whilst variety shows on television, soap operas, drama, etc., are understood as being mimetic; fictions which entertain. Audiences are aware of this and it is because of this that we are likely to judge media products on the basis of how "realistic" they are, which makes us forget that they are only constructs, and not real at all. Although news, documentaries, etc., deal with fact, the facts are mediated by reporters, camera technicians, directors, producers and others. Although the media products might be factual and informative, they are still only constructed versions of the real world.

By studying how the media are produced, therefore, we can increase our understanding of how the media "get their message across" and what effects the production methods have on these messages.

Try this for yourself: find a photograph which shows some kind of action happening between several different people. Take two pieces of paper and cover up parts of your photograph so that it "tells a different story" to the original one. Write a new caption for the picture which you have made.

Summary of the main points raised in this chapter.

Semiology is the study of signs and forms part of the "language" used to analyse media products. You will use semiological terms quite naturally during the course of your studies. Semiology is a "way of looking" at the world which presupposes that we actively make meaning from our world and, therefore, that the viewer/listener/reader, etc., has an active part to play in understanding media texts.

The mass media are organised into industries and institutions which means that a variety of experts produce different media and that media products are dependant on finance from a variety of sources such as advertising revenue, licence fees, etc.

The intended audiences for the messages produced by the media vary in relation to age, gender and class which makes audiences complex in nature.

Media messages are constructed to inform and/or entertain an audience but the media can also persuade.

The methods used to make media messages will vary in relation to the particular media being constructed. Newspaper production, for example, demands differents sets of expertise from other media forms. It is important to study how various media are produced because this allows us to see that methods of production can alter the "truth".

Notes

1. Argyle, Michael, *Bodily Communication*, Methuen, London, (1975), page 78.

2. Stuart Hood, in his book *On Television*, Pluto Press, 1983, page 33, states:

   "A television complex like the BBC's Television Centre is an electronic factory in which the production (or manufacture) of television programmes is organized on industrial lines. The same rules apply to its running and management as to the management of an industrial plant of comparable size and complexity . . . The same management techniques are applied as are used in a car factory or in a factory producing television sets."

3. Root, Jane, *Open the Box*, Comedia, London, (1986), page 52.

CHAPTER THREE

STUDYING MASS MEDIA FOR HIGHER GRADE CANDIDATES

(i)   The Course

If you are studying all the specified areas for the current Higher Grade exam — Film, Narrative and Representations — you can expect to spend anything up to 15 to 20 hours of class time on mass media and a similar amount of time in home study. Twenty hours, or less, in the classroom is not a great deal of time, and the range and variety of media which can be dealt with in the classroom is likely to be restricted because of this.

I would suggest, therefore, that you attempt to apply the ideas which you will encounter during class time to viewing/listening/reading, etc., at home. You will find that the more effort you invest this way, the more you are likely to gain from it.

You must remember, however, that this should not be to the detriment of other areas of study such as poetry, prose or drama .

(ii)   Why should we bother to study the media?

The Joint Working Party Report concerning the Revised Higher and CSYS Examinations contains the following statement:

> The mass media have a major influence on our lives. Increasingly they offer our students some of their most profound communicative and aesthetic experiences."

The Examination Board acknowledge, therefore, that the media form an important part of human social experience and that it is worth understanding about mass media because of this. The Report continues by pointing out that teachers of English have, for many years now, been including aspects of media studies in the English syllabus. For example, you may have looked closely at the language and structure of newspaper articles, been asked to write an article in the style of a quality, or popular newspaper; examined the characters in a soap opera; discussed topics in class concerning the media such as violence on television; or have participated in other activities involving either examining, or making, a media product.

The extent to which such activities have entered English classrooms has, therefore, also been acknowledged by the Examination Board, ultimately, by providing students with the opportunity to demonstrate their knowledge and interest during an exam.

(iii)   Three areas of study

Three areas of study have been prescribed by the Scottish Examination Board (up to and including 1992). These are: *Film*, *Narrative* and *Representations*. Questions on these areas will appear under the "Mass Media" section of the Writing Paper (Paper II) in the English Higher Grade examinations. Sample questions from previous years can be found in Chapter Seven of this guide, together with advice about how to answer questions.

The following chapters on Film, Narrative and Representations are intended to assist students towards an understanding of the ideas and terms used in the Board's guidelines.

Summary of the main points raised in this chapter

The Scottish Examination Board have suggested that approximately 15 to 20 hours of class time should be devoted to mass media with a similar amount of time being spent in home study. You should, therefore, be prepared to apply the ideas which you encounter during class time to your private viewing/ listening/reading, etc. You should not, however, neglect other areas of your English course.

The areas of study for Mass Media (up to and including 1992) are: Film, Narrative and Representations.

CHAPTER FOUR

FILM

Look at Figure 2 and you will see the main areas suggested for Film study in the Higher Grade Examinations.

Figure 2

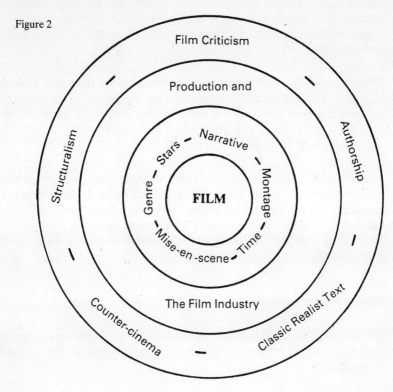

These have been placed within a matrix of three circles to make them easier to locate. The centre of the circle, closest to the word "Film", involves the student in looking closely at films as finished products. The middle circle concentrates on film production and the film industry. The outermost circle concerns ways of looking at film which means that we should know some of the theories which inform film criticism. The information in this chapter is organised accordingly.

c

(i)   Looking at Films as finished products

(a)   Telling the story

One of the most important aspects of film making is establishing a narrative. This means that everyone involved in making the film must contribute something towards "telling the story": the director, the actors and actresses, the costume designers, the make-up artists, the people who design and build the film sets, the lighting, camera and sound technicians, and the many others who are involved, help to construct the story.

Constructing the story, however, involves more than the collecting together of a huge number of experts. (Successful films have been made on low budgets with only a few people involved.) What is more important is technical expertise and the ability to make a convincing construct which an audience can believe in.

We will begin by looking at narrative structure before moving to the various elements within the structure which make a film unique. The narrative structure could be likened to a film's bare "skeleton", whilst the other elements which make a film unique could be likened to the flesh, skin and other features which cover the skeleton. (See Chapter Five: Narrative; 'plot' and 'story'.)

(b)   Kinds of narrative structure

There are different kinds of narrative structure. The most common structure is the "classic" structure which contains the following elements:

1.   Events will be organised on a strictly linear basis beginning with a "normal" state, sometimes called equilibrium, which will be disrupted in some way, then resolved, before returning to a previous or new state of equilibrium.

2.   A problem will be posed which creates the disruption and the problem will be solved in some way, leaving us with a definite and satisfactory ending. (A return to equilibrium.)

34

3. The characters will be "real" and we will be able to believe easily in them and identify with them.

4. The settings (time and place) can be easily understood or recognised.

This is the most common form of narrative structure and is likely to be the kind of structure which you will study.

There are alternative narrative structures which differ fundamentally from the classic structure in the following ways:

1. The events in the film will not follow a strictly linear path. Some or all of the following will appear in the organisation of the narrative structure: interruptions to the story, digressions from the story, repetitiousness and information which is not strictly necessary to the telling of the story.

2. The story may not end satisfactorily: we may be left with unanswered questions.

3. The characters may seem incredible. We may not be able to easily identify with them or believe in them.

4. The setting of the story may change without explanation.

This is a simplified version of what might happen outside the classic narrative structure. (See "counter-cinema" later in this chapter (page 46).)

(c)   *Other elements in film narrative*

In this section, we will be examining how film narrative is put together and, in the process of doing so, some of the language of film making.

On the following page are some of the basic methods used in

narrative construction. Take careful note of the language used:

Montage

Montage is the name given to the process of moving from one picture to another and is one of the most basic methods of story telling in film. Pictures following each other tell a story. For example, a famous Russian film-maker called Pudovkin tried an experiment with the still image of a man's face. He took two pictures of a man's face which were exactly the same: the face was quite expressionless. Next to one of the pictures he put a bowl of food. Next to the other he put a graveyard. When the people who took part in the experiment were questioned about the pairs of photographs, they nearly always said that the face next to the bowl of food was showing hunger and the face next to the graveyard was showing sadness. Unusual if you bear in mind that the face was totally expressionless!

A further example of how montage works comes from another great film director, Eisenstein, who put conflicting pictures beside each other to produce certain emotional responses from the audience. An example of this idea would be a close up of a gun barrel next to a terrified face. The audience would "add" these two images together to make the emotion "fear".

Montage, therefore, is a complex process which involves a fair amount of artistic and technical knowledge. It is argued that it is just as much an art to construct film **shots** and **soundtrack** into the coherent whole which we call a "film" as it is to paint a picture or write a novel. An artist who uses oil colours requires technical knowledge to mix colours and lay them on the canvas but the finished result is more to do with creativity. Films involve similar creative talents. The director's "palet", however consists of a mixture of sound effects, dialogue, music, **camera angles**, colour definition and lighting and the many other important parts of a film. (See "authorship" later in this chapter (page 45).)

As an exercise in montage, look carefully at one of the many television commercials which "tell a story". Try to decide how montage helps you to understand the story.

Can you think of any other ideas which would be similar to Pudovkin's or Eisenstein's ideas?

Time

Telling the story in cinematic terms involves the manipulation of **time** and **space** on film. Montage helps this process. Through montage, we can cover twenty years in a few seconds by juxtapositioning pictures of events in someone's life. We can be in two places at once or move thousands of miles in a few seconds by merely putting a series of pictures together.

Think, for example, of the *actual* time it would take to show your journey to school, college or work. You might walk a few hundred yards to a bus stop; wait there for a few minutes; board the bus when it arrives and travel for several minutes before alighting and walking for a further five minutes. This sequence could take seconds on film by using the techniques of montage. You could be shown leaving your house, boarding a bus and alighting at your destination with a final shot of you entering your school, college or workplace. A twenty minute journey, therefore, can be implied to the viewer over a period, on film, of only two minutes. (Although, obviously, it could take some hours to film a sequence such as this, bearing in mind that you would have to set up and dismantle equipment and travel the physical distances involved!)

The length of time we are allowed to look at a picture is also important. A series of pictures of only a few seconds' duration can give the impression of urgency, or movement, or speed. Similarly, shots of the same subject over a long duration of time can give the opposite impression.

It is important to bear in mind that, as previously mentioned, films are not made in one continuous sequence. The whole effect of a film, i.e. the combination of pictures and sound is the result of many hours of work at the **editing** stage when the director will work with several other people to decide which shots are most effective to produce the desired emotion, or visual effect.

After you have given the ideas discussed above some thought, using your own experiences of film, think of an example of how time and space were manipulated in a film you have seen and/or of how the juxtapositioning of sequences of images produced emotion such as fear, pleasure or joy. Explain how you think this was achieved.

Mise-en-scene

We are now going to explore a further important aspect of story telling called **mise-en-scene**. (This is a French term meaning "putting it in the scene" or, in cinematic terms, "to put on the screen".)

Directors and set designers think carefully about what they will include "in the scene" on film. Each item which the audience sees inside the **frame** of a picture will make meaning. Early in Chapter One, I said that:

> "We have a habit of constructing, or making, meaning for ourselves from the everyday things which we come across in our society. For example, if we walk down a busy street in town, we will see people, shop windows, cars, traffic signs, and a host of other things which will be meaningful. By looking at their clothing, their age, bearing and facial expression, we can categorise people into old, young, fashionable, dowdy, kind, beautiful or ugly." (Page 6.)

This same process takes place when we watch the action on a cinema screen. We will make meaning from a character's clothes, bearing and expression. We will absorb information from the surroundings which the character has been placed in and we will create meaning from what we understand about these things.

We rarely acknowledge this process of meaning-making either in everyday life or when we are watching a film but the subtle influence of what is "in the scene" can support the process of story telling in the cinema.

Again, in Chapter Two, I mentioned how we "read" meaning into images:

> "When we go to the cinema to watch a film, we begin decoding the messages on the screen immediately the film begins . . . We watch the images on the screen and decide where and when the action is taking place . . . lighting . . .

38

can reveal much about the subject and mood . . . Dark lighting will produce a "creepy" or gloomy mood. Bright lighting . . . is likely to have the opposite effect." (Page 17.)

Mise-en-scene, therefore, not only includes props, characters and background, but the kind of lighting which has been used. Each of these combine to create pictures inside a frame.

Cinematic film is a strip of celluloid and if you have loaded a role of film into your camera and taken photographs, you have been working with similar materials to the film used in cinematography. The negatives used to make your prints each contain a "frame" within which your picture has been composed. Cinematic films work on a similar principal except that they consist of a *series* of images which photograph small pieces of continuous action. When all of the frames are played through a projector at high speed, they produce the illusion of movement.

An amusing way of reproducing similar effects for yourself is to take a thick notebook and carefully draw a matchstick man in the bottom corner of each page, changing the leg and arm positions fractionally with each drawing. After this, lift the pages with your thumb and let them drop rapidly one after the other. Your matchstick man will now appear to be moving his arms and legs. This effect is called "constancy of vision" and is created by our brain and eyes working together to produce the illusion of movement because they cannot process information quickly enough. Although we know that each matchstick man is on a separate piece of paper, the rapid movement of the pages deceives our eyes into believing otherwise and we "see" him "moving".

Each separate image on the film is inside a frame. Film, therefore, is two-dimensional — each image is flat — but played through the projector, the images seem to become three-dimensional: we know that we are looking at a flat screen but our eyes will note things like the positioning and angle of floors, walls and ceilings which will give us an impression of space and depth, all of which help to create mise-en-scene.

An example of how carefully mise-en-scene is constructed can be seen in the film *1984* which is based on George Orwell's novel of the same title. The lighting throughout the film produces dull, shadowy, almost **monochrome** effects and in this way adds to the gloomy atmosphere which pervades the characters' lives.

The sets have also been carefully prepared. One small detail from the set helps to illustrate this. In the novel, the narrative begins: "It was a bright cold day in April, and the clocks were striking thirteen . . ." This seems odd to us because most clocks which strike the hour (Big Ben, for example) only strike the hour up to twelve o'clock and then they begin again at one o'clock. The set designer, however, has interpreted this for us by designing a clock face which is numbered from 1 to 24, thus providing a reason why the clocks might strike thirteen.

Although this clever visual detail helps to recreate on screen the images created first of all by Orwell in print, perhaps you would like to give some thought to how seeing a detail like this affects how we might now interpret this idea from Orwell's novel. Does the screen image of the clock create the same feeling of things being wrong as the first sentence in the novel? Try to give a reason for your feelings about this.

As a further exercise, try taking special note of the mise-en-scene of any future films which you watch. What is in the background of the picture? What kind of objects are contained within the picture frame? What lighting is used — **high-** or **low-key**? What do the characters wear?

(d)   *Film genre*

Like novels, films fall into different categories, or **genres**. If a film is of a particular genre, this means that it is similar to others of its kind. Studying genre, therefore, involves looking at the similarities and differences which occur between films within one or more genres.

As I explained earlier (see (iii) Rules and Conventions of Construction, page 19) films (like other media) are produced according to certain rules or conventions. When we place a film within a certain genre, we are acknowledging that the film follows the rules and conventions of its kind; patterns will emerge in the film which reflect similarities to other films of that type. For example, similarities in character, setting, narrative and theme.

Male characters in Westerns are likely to be heroic, lone figures, who are in conflict with social or personal circumstances brought about by the geographical location and era of the setting which films of the Western genre share, i.e. the "wild" West of America around the end of the last century.

Consider for a moment what you would expect to see in the type of film we call a "Western". Would there be cowboys? Gunfighting? Cattle rustling or bank robberies? Red Indians? Settlers in wagon-trains? What kind of story would it be? What kind of characters would you see? How would they be dressed? How would they behave?

What would you expect to find in a horror film? Strange characters? Blood? Special effects? Creepy music? Low-key lighting?

Because we tend to categorise films, and readily recognise the various ingredients which should appear in a particular genre, our enjoyment is enhanced by our expectations. When audiences go to the cinema expecting to see a Western, with all the trimmings of rough cowboy heroes, gunfights, brawls and cattle-rustling, they might be disappointed if they found that the story had been entirely set within a ranch house and featured a domestic crisis mostly enacted in the sitting room!

Genre studies have identified a variety of forms in mainstream cinema over the past few years. Brief details of some of the main film genres are given below:

The Western

Typically, these films are set in the "wild" West of America, near the end of the last century. The film is likely to be concerned with the hardships experienced by early settlers on the American frontier, the struggles of the threatened Red Indian populations, and the dichotomy between "East" and "West" (civilisation and wilderness).

The heroic male figure struggling to assert himself amid all the hardships of the West is a common figure in these films. Criminal activities often feature, with the male figure as perpetrator.

41

Women are often stereotypical: the open-hearted worldly-wise "fallen woman" who frequents the male domain of the saloon bar often features in the Western. This stereotype can be compared with the honest, hard-working and virtuous wife/mother figure.

Adventure

The adventure film is epitomised by the element of danger and excitement present in the film. These films usually share exotic locations and a male hero figure who overcomes all the physical and psychological dangers with which he is confronted during the course of the narrative.

Science Fiction

If the Western is concerned with the American frontier of the last century, then science fiction is typically concerned with the frontiers of outer space in the future. The invasion of earth from outer space or exploration of outer space from earth are common themes in these films.

Horror

European literary traditions (e.g. the Victorian gothic novel) have helped to shape the kind of horror film which relies for effect on werewolves, the mythical European location of Count Dracula's Transylvania, Frankenstein's indestructible monster and creepy graveyards lit by the eerie glow of the full moon. These traditional sources of horror, however, have been eclipsed by the more recent psychological or sociological horrors of, e.g. *Psycho* or *Halloween*. *Psycho* is a classic horror movie of the kind which uses psychological twists and turns to keep the viewer guessing and *Halloween* introduces horror into the "normal" American family home.

These, of course, are only a few of many film genres. Understanding genre entails close analysis of characters, themes, narrative and iconography of the film (i.e. recurrent images in genre films such as dress, settings, or the physical attributes of the main characters). By "reading" the film in this way, we can categorise film according to their conventions of construction.

(e)   The star system

Film stars are an important ingredient in many films and many of us have our favourite film stars whom we avidly follow, going to the cinema whenever a new film appears with this person in the starring role.

The star system first began in the early days of film making at the beginning of this century when particular studios were known to make certain kinds of films, e.g., Hammer Studios became famous for their horror films. Accompanying the studio system, came the star system, with actors and actresses contracted to studios which often developed similar roles especially for the same actor or actress. Peter Cushing, for example, became linked with horror movies such as *Dracula* and *Frankenstein's Monster* made by Hammer Studios. Cushing remained with the studio for many years, only leaving when they changed their film genre to satisfy new demands from audiences.

Stars, then, are often linked with film genre. This happens, usually, because the actor or actress takes a leading role in a film which turns out to be a box office success. This, in turn, makes that person an extremely marketable product. When the person stars in a new film, it is likely that more money will be asked from audiences at the box-office. If the actor or actress is lucky enough to have several such successes, their immediate future is assured as they will be in further demand to star in films because it will be assumed that their presence in a starring role will assure box-office success.

(f)   Ideologies

Ideologies are not "things". They are lived and shared experiences by members of society. They are abstract rather than concrete and because the shared beliefs, ideas and habits of thought which make ideologies are very much part of our way of life, we rarely think about them.

43

All media can be studied in terms of the dominant ideologies which they contain. The "social message" which is present in a film could be based, amongst other things, on such considerations as class, culture, politics and the place of the individual in society depending on race, gender, age, etc.

You are unlikely to find the social and cultural message of a film without looking at the deeper meanings contained within, for example, the framework of character, setting and plot. The audience "make meaning" by "reading" the total film, a process called *diegesis*.

(ii)   Production and the film industry

Like all media products, film is constructed and the previous sections have dealt with some of the ingredients commonly found in films. What you see on a cinema screen has, therefore, been very carefully put together by a number of experts in the field of film making which creates a product specifically produced to sell in the film market place, i.e. to cinema distribution agencies at home and abroad. This section deals with these points.

It should never be forgotten that the films which we see in the cinema are usually the result of a huge financial investment. There are, however, exceptions to the rule and "low-budget" films have been known to reach the big screen. Films which have cost millions to make are not always the most successful and several films which have had millions invested in their making have been box office flops.

For many years, the Hollywood conglomerates have dominated the market place, producing classics like *Gone with the Wind*, which has been estimated to have earned, over a period of fifty years, $840 million dollars (an estimate based on modern-day dollar equivalents[1]).

We must remember, however, that not all films are made for the cinema. Television companies sometimes commission films or contribute to their making. One example of this kind of backing was the Scottish Producer Mike Radford's *Another Time, Another Place*, based on the novel by the Scottish writer, Jessie Kesson. This film was jointly financed by Rediffusion Films, Channel Four and the Scottish Arts[2].

44

Since films are made to "sell" to the "audience-consumers" and cost money to make, it can be a difficult task to persuade possible financiers to part with their money. The usual steps in this process are: *(a)* coming up with an idea; *(b)* putting together a "package"; *(c)* making a business deal for financial backing.

The producer or director who has come up with his idea for a film (possibly an adaptation of a novel such as Orwell's *1984* and Kesson's *Another Time, Another Place*, or a play or an original **screenplay**) must put his or her idea over in attractive terms, i.e. make the film sound like a feasible project, decide in advance how much money would be required, taking into account possible "starring" roles, location and the many other items which would add to the cost and then "sell" this "package" for financial backing.

(iii)   Film criticism

James Monaco, in his textbook *How to Read a Film*, asks the following questions: "How do we determine cinematic value? How do we know what's 'symbolic of junk'? . . . Are there any true universal "rules" for film art? What does film do? What are its limits?" Monaco identifies questions like these as being important to film theory and criticism.

Film criticism looks at films from a variety of viewpoints — as works of art, genre, social statements, etc. In this final section on Film, I will discuss, in brief, some of the main critical approaches to film.

Authorship

In **authorship** (*also known as* **auteur**), a film is attributed to the person who made it, i.e. the "author". The film, therefore, is criticised on the basis of the distinctive craft of a particular film director, e.g. Alfred Hitchcock became well-known for his psychological thrillers. Many recurrent themes can be found in Hitchcock's films such as guilt, split identity, obsession and other ideas which make them distinctly Hitchcock's films. Many film critics and theorists have written about Hitchcock's films, demonstrating their distinction which is attributed to the "art" of the film director.

45

Classic realist text

The ideas in this theory form part of a debate which is still continuing. Colin MacCabe, who is the author of this theory, sees realist — or classic — narrative as problematic. We the audience are, according to this theory, manipulated into believing that what we see on the cinema screen is a form of "reality" when, in fact, it is a construct of reality which only reinforces dominant ideologies of our culture. This idea moves away from theories which treat film as a reflection of the real world and throws into dispute audience point of view. This theory argues that when we go to the cinema, we passively accept what we see because the classic narrative structure requires no real thought. The story is told from beginning to end and we, the audience do not require to engage with it — we merely watch, or "consume". By concentrating on narrative structure, however, all films become reduced to a strict formula — a rigidity which ignores other constants such as themes which could be seen to be, in some cases, more important than plot.

Counter-cinema

You are now familiar with what classic film narrative means (see page 34 and above). The classic narrative text works by constructing an illusion of reality. Counter-cinema, as its name suggests, opposes the classic realist text by breaking down the codes of cinema which create this illusory reality. The intention behind this is to demonstrate that life is simply not like that.

The characters in classic realist films take part in a chronological sequence of events which are meant to assist the audience watching the film to understand the narrative; to encourage a "willing suspension of disbelief". The theory of counter-cinema is that the celluloid world created in the cinema (and representing dominant ideologies) should be questioned, challenged and contradicted.

Films which could be classed as counter-cinema, therefore, might disrupt the classic sequence of events by interrupting the narrative with images which are intrusive or by making the characters question their own actions. In this way, a cinema experience is created which estranges the audience and makes them question what they see rather than, as in classic realist film, carries them along without the need to think too much.

The main elements of counter-cinema have been identified by Peter Wollen[3] and are shown below next to the elements of classic cinema which they oppose:

Classic Cinema	Counter-cinema
Narrative transitivity	Narrative intransitivity
Identification	Estrangement
Transparency	Foregrounding
Single diegesis	Multiple diegesis
Closure	Aperture
Pleasure	Unpleasure
Fiction	Reality

Some of the more difficult terms are explained below:

Narrative transitivity = linear movement of the narrative (from beginning to end). Intransitivity, therefore, means that the story will not follow a logical sequence.

Identification = the audience can easily identify with the characters and situations. Estrangement, therefore, means that the characters are distanced from the audience.

Transparency = nothing stands in the way of the audience's understanding and enjoyment of the story. Foregrounding, therefore, causes the opposite effect. By, for example, using camera movements which are contrary to what the audience might expect in a particular situation, the camera movements impinge on the action, disrupting the flow of the narrative.

Closure = the audience is encouraged by a number of narrative devices to "read" the narrative in a particular way. Aperture, therefore, means that the narrative is "open" and may be understood in a number of different ways. This may make the audience feel dissatisfied because we are used to stories which have a high degree of "closure".

The contribution of structuralist thought to theories of film are most obvious in discussions about narrative. What is structuralism? It is a complex set of theories which encompasses semiology amongst other ideas. To enter into a discussion about the origins and history of structuralism would be counter-productive at this point. So, we will make this explanation as simple as possible. Throughout this guide, I have taken the point of view that you the reader — or we, the audience — "make meaning" from signs and codes. If we take this idea and apply it to film narrative, we can "strip down" film narrative into its component parts, thus making clear how the film was constructed. Structuralist thought always presupposes that there is an underlying "structure" in film.

Summary of the main points raised in this chapter

Film, for the purposes of the Higher English course on Mass Media, should be examined from three inter-dependent points of view:

1. Film as finished product;
2. Film production and the film industry;
3. Critical approaches used by film theorists.

1. Film as a finished product looks at film narrative and how it is produced; the language used to describe this process — montage, time, mise-en-scene; the categorisation of film (film genre); the star system; the cultural and social aspects of film (ideologies).

2. The section, Production and the film industry, discusses film as a marketable product which begins as an idea which is "sold" for financial backing.

3. The section, Film criticism, provides a brief overview of the main theories of film criticism: authorship, classic realist text, counter-cinema and structuralism.

Notes

1. Adrian Turner, *A Celebration of Gone with the Wind*, A Dragon's World Book, London and New York.

2. From information contained in the booklet on the film *Another Time, Another Place*, published by Film Education in association with the Scottish Film Council and the Association for Media Education in Scotland.

3. Peter Wollen, 'Counter-cinema: *ven d'est*', *Afterimage* No. 4, 1972 in Pam Cook (Ed), *The Cinema Book*, British Film Institute 1985.

CHAPTER FIVE

NARRATIVE

You will now understand, from your readings on film, some of the complexities involved in creating narrative. Film narrative is sustained through the efforts of many people and although the basic ingredients of narrative do not differ fundamentally from the traditional elements which you would expect to find in a novel, i.e. setting, character, conflict and resolution, the finished product is quite different and audience expectations and responses are different.

"Plot" and "Story"

When we discuss literature, we are likely to talk about the "plot" of a novel or play. The plot, of course, is the plan of events which gives the work its overall shape. I mentioned earlier that Film Narrative can be sub-divided into "narrative structures" and "other elements". Narrative structure can be seen as equivalent to the "plot", i.e. the linear events which move from disruption to resolution. The other elements of narrative relate to how the story is told, e.g. "Once upon a time . . .". We expect, therefore, to be taken on a small journey from A to B when we read a story, watch a play, or watch a film.

Narrative, therefore, always implies movement. Todorov[1], a structuralist, argues that:

> ". . . all narrative is a movement between two equilibriums which are similar but not identical. At the start of the narrative, there is always a stable situation; the characters form a configuration which can shift but which nonetheless keeps a certain number of fundamental features intact . . . something occurs which introduces a disequilibrium (or, one might say, a negative equilibrium) . . . At the end of the story, the equilibrium is then re-established but is is no longer that of the beginning."

This idea can be illustrated graphically as shown on the following page.

Narrative

story begins: →→→ something occurs: →→→ story ends.

(stable situation
or "equilibrium") (causes upset or
"disequilibrium") (*different* stable
situation restored)

The most important points about this model of narrative are that 1. Narrative represents movement and 2. That the stable situation (or point of equilibrium) at the end of the story will be different to the stable situation at the beginning of the story. Narrative is seen in this model, therefore, to be linear and it is a suitable model for talking about the plot of most novels, plays and films.

Narrative and the media

Narrative can be found across the media spectrum and not only in film. Furthermore, narrative need not relate only to fiction. Factual accounts such as documentaries, news programmes, and television or radio series which deal with factual matters, have narratives.

In these cases, narrative requires to be studied in context, i.e. by making close reference to the **text** being studied. This is important, because only by studying the text in question can you find out the various devices used to "tell the story".

Television

Television, for example, uses similar codes and conventions to film because these media involve image and sound. Television narrative is constructed, like film narrative, by employing codes such as **camera angles**, **lighting**, **framing**, **editing**, etc. The medium of television, however, is different from film. A television screen, for example, is much smaller than a cinema screen. Often, cameras are used to televise "*live*" on location which means that editing cannot be carried out. Instead of editing, several cameras are used — for example, at the bottom, middle and top of a football pitch — which allows the production team to switch cameras, live, to various points of the action being televised.

Although narrative, therefore, can be found in television, there are distinctive differences between film and television narrative.

Film Narrative	*Television Narrative*
Usually linear, i.e. tells the story from beginning to end.	Often open-ended or circular in nature.
Characters usually become altered in some way during the course of the story so that they rarely end up in the same state as they were at the beginning of the film.	Repetitious — often the same characters, e.g. this most obviously applies to soap operas, news and games shows.

The most powerful feature of any narrative is the very human wish to keep watching, reading or listening until we know what happens next. How do you feel, for example, if you are watching your favourite programme on television and you are called away from the television set to answer the telephone? You feel annoyed. You feel annoyed because you are going to be denied one of the gratifications or pleasures of narrative — you are being denied the resolution of the narrative **hook** or **enigma** which keeps us riveted to our seats: by answering the phone, you will not find out what happens next.

Open-ended narrative

Police series are a good example of the fact that there is often no real resolution to television narrative. There have been many police series on television over the years. One current T.V. serial, as I write this, is *The Bill*, which is shown twice weekly on I.T.V. The same main characters are seen every week and deal with different problems related to policing our society: murder, dishonesty, police hatred and racism have all featured in this series. Although there will be a resolution of the immediate problem featured in any one particular episode of the serial, we know that by the next episode, the central enigma — crime in society — will not have been resolved and we will have the pleasure of watching yet another episode. The main characters are unlikely to have changed a great deal; they maintain distinct and unique characteristics throughout the duration of the serial — which makes them seem like "real" people.

52

Games shows, news programmes, soap operas, serials, documentaries: all of these, and more, are repetitious in nature. We expect to see the same newsreader reading the news each evening; it is quite comforting to see the same faces on television. Continuity is maintained in this way.

Not only do we see the same faces, but we are likely to see our favourite programme in the same time-slot each week. We become annoyed if the programme controller has the cheek to move our favourite game show to a different time slot in order to accommodate something which is seen to be of more immediate value such as live coverage of football or of a news programme about a national or international disaster!

The same kind of narrative hook applies to news programmes. The authoritative voice of the newsreader "tells us the story", i.e. narrates. We believe implicitly in this voice. The tone and pacing of the newsreader's words are significant: the words spoken are meant to be believed and are extremely serious in nature.

The news invariably begins in the same way, with **headlines**. Immediately, we are hooked. We want to know what happens next and we will listen until we find out. We watch and listen until the end of the news programme in order to find out about today's news but we know that there will be more news. The central enigma — world news — is never resolved because something different is happening every minute of every day. We will, therefore, watch the next "episode" either later that day or the next day, and the next, and so on.

Narrative in still images

Still images, especially news photographs and the photographic images used in advertising, are capable of "telling a story".

Women's magazines, for example, are full of colour images related to beauty, fashion, cookery and advertisements. Women are likely to associate themselves with the subjects of the photographs in the same way that we might associate ourselves with the key character in a novel or film. An image of a woman, for example, frozen in the act of sipping a drink implies that there is a "before" and "after" to this image. Presumably, she has lifted the drink to her lips before being photographed in the position which is displayed in the photograph and, presumably, she will follow the action through by drinking from the glass. Any words which appear alongside the image will **anchor** the meaning, either confirming, or adding to, the story contained in the image.

News photographs work in a similar way. For example, a photograph of a man standing on the ledge of a building high above street level, together with the caption: "Tense minutes before P.C. MacLean coaxes Mr. Smith back inside" implies a narrative. The man has inched his way along the ledge and his image is captured by the photographer before a policeman manages to rescue him and bring him back inside the building.

Try to find examples of a variety of narratives, e.g. television serials, soap operas, news programmes, documentaries, photographs from advertising or news reporting, and attempt to show how these "tell a story".

Summary of the main points raised in this chapter

Narrative can be understood in terms of "plot" and "story".

Narrative always implies movement, usually consisting of a state of equilibrium which is disrupted before being restored to a new state of equilibrium.

Narrative can be found in many different media forms.

Narrative applies to both fact and fiction, e.g. television news and documentaries; soap operas, games shows.

54

Each media text should be studied closely in order to reveal which particular narrative devices have been employed by those who constructed it.

Television narrative does not differ fundamentally from that of film, except that television narrative tends to be open-ended and repetitive in nature.

Still images, especially those connected with advertising and news reporting, often imply narrative content.

Notes

1.   Tzvetan Todorov, *The Fantastic*, Cornell University Press, (1975).

CHAPTER SIX

REPRESENTATIONS

The word **representations** is used whenever we want to discuss how groups of people, nations or events are "represented" in the media. The following idea might help to demonstrate what is meant by this.

You will probably know that someone who is employed to sell a company's products is called a "representative". Very often a company is judged on the basis of how efficient that person is. Something similar happens when young people, or the elderly, or a nation are featured in the media. Certain common ways of showing these become accepted as a representation of *all* young people, or the elderly, or of a whole nation.

Think for a moment about how Scotland is often represented on television. White heather? Highland cattle? Thistles? Kilts? Is Scotland *really* like this or do the media choose to show certain things about Scotland which makes other countries think of us in a particular way?

Here are some questions which you might like to ask yourself about representations:

Who makes representations?

How are representations made?

Who are the representations aimed at?

(i)   Who makes representations?

All media play a part in making representations. Perhaps the most powerful are those media which employ not only written or aural methods such as newspapers or radio but those which also deploy visual methods such as film, television and the advertising industry. These industries have the ability to construct reality in a much more effective way than written texts, or sound, would allow because they are able to support their **construct** with pictures. In this way familiar objects, scenes and characters can be deployed so that television, film or advertising images are made to seem like "reflections" of the world instead of the imaginative and clever constructions of the world which they are.

Study as many television advertisements as you can which feature families. You are likely to find that the family forms a neat unit, e.g. "mummy, daddy and two children" who all get on wonderfully well together. What kind of home do they share? What would you say about their financial position in life? What impression do they give about "the family" in Britain?

(ii) How are representations made?

The problems inherent in the idea of representations arise because the media present their constructs as "reality". A television play, for example, is often judged on the basis of how "real" the characters or the setting seem. We tend to criticise media output when it does not reach audience expectations of reality. It is easy, therefore, to fall into the trap of believing that all people who live in London speak with a cockney accent or that all football supporters are rowdies who vandalise their surroundings and assault people.

I have already mentioned that all media play a part in making representations. When examining representations of, for example, teenagers, therefore, you should be prepared to look for representations of teenagers across a variety of media. Taking all the "bits and pieces" of information you find in print, video, film, etc., you will see various examples of the abstract idea of "teenager" emerging. How often are the same examples repeated? What effect is this likely to have on the people who are exposed to these representations?

For example, *Taggart* epitomises the "tough cop". He *stands for* the typical detective who, like the Canadian Mounties, "always gets his man". Taggart is at odds with his superiors, his colleagues and his family. He is totally devoted to his job which comes before everything else in his life. This same dedication to duty can be found across a whole spectrum of police series, both American and British. The "tough man" image can also be found across that same spectrum. The "them" and "me" situation where the policeman is at loggerheads with authority and/or his colleagues can also be found.

These situations and behaviour, therefore, become a kind of shorthand for police detectives in television and film; audiences are familiar with these ideas and because of this, the image of the "typical cop" becomes a quick and efficient method of helping to get the story across.

Representations are formulated from what is understood to be typical about individuals, groups and nations.

(iii)   Who are the representations aimed at?

The audience for media representations are the public. We are all exposed to a variety of media during our day to day existence in our society. Exactly which section of the public representations are aimed at will depend on the purpose of the communication, e.g. advertising, film, television.

Often, audiences themselves become representations when programme-makers get to work. By aiming particular programmes at particular audiences, e.g. a women's magazine programme broadcast on television at 10.30 a.m. is likely to contain themes and ideas which the programme-makers think will interest the typical housewife. In this way, audiences are created by the programme-makers and programmes are tailored to what it is thought that the audience will like.

Negotiating meanings

Media representations work as the result of a process which draws on social and cultural values. Audiences then "read" these values. This means that we are likely to take a viewpoint which reflects our own social values as well as the values of the society we live in. We are likely, therefore, to make "readings" of media constructs by either accepting them, accepting them with reservations, or rejecting them outright. These three basic ideas are related to what have been called [1] **dominant codes**, **negotiated codes** and **oppositional codes**.

The media are likely to take up a point of view which reflects the *dominant* ideological position of the majority. If the audience for, lets say, a television programme about the importance of the state system of education share the dominant values being broadcast, then all is well — they will accept what they see and hear as a reflection of their own values.

If, however, the audience for that same programme happen to be people who see the value of state education but would also be prepared to argue for private education, then this changes that audience's "reading". Because they can see the value of state education but hold their own point of view, they accept the dominant values but would wish to *negotiate* for their own values.

Advocates of home education, i.e. people in society who actively support teaching children at home and neither send them to state schools nor private schools would *oppose* the ideas in the programme, dismissing them outright.

To put this more simply, imagine you are having a conversation with your parents, and your brother and sister. You are discussing whether or not teenagers should be allowed to please themselves about what time they arrive home at night.

Your parents are adamant that young people should not be allowed to stay out as long as they wish. Furthermore, they insist that this is the point of view which is held by every responsible adult with whom they have discussed this question. (They represent the *dominant* codes because their ideas are shared by many people).

Your sister and you can understand why your parents hold this point of view but feel that there should be occasions when young people should be allowed to make up their own mind — for example, when going to a party which may only begin to get interesting at the very moment you have promised to leave for home. (You represent the *negotiated* codes because you can appreciate the ideas behind the dominant viewpoint but you wish to negotiate your own ideas.)

Your brother, who is older than your sister and you, thinks that young people should not be restricted in their movements and that no promises should be extracted from them to be home at a particular time of night. (He represents the *oppositional* codes because he is totally opposed to the dominant values shared by many people.)

Sometimes, the media create highly simplified representations, taking broad generalisations about people or nations, and applying these to characters or situations in order to get a message across to an audience very quickly. For example, stereotyping is often used in comedy. People and situations are stereotyped in order to create humour. I have used some cartoons to illustrate this point. You can see these below and in the worksheets which follow.

What makes it funny?

Stereotypes in Cartoons

Cartoons often rely on our knowledge of stereotypes. Many cartoons would not be funny if we did not understand about the generalisations in the pictures and words used in the cartoon.

The cartoon shown below in Figure 3 relies on our understanding of two things:

1. A stereotypical image of Americans as boastful, i.e. "Everything's bigger and better in America".

Figure 3

" He was bragging about how everything's so much bigger in the States— then he met your mother!"

2.   A stereotypical image of mothers-in-law as ugly, bossy or likely to take over or overstay their welcome in the son-or-daughter-in-law's home. In this case, the ugly mother-in-law stereotype has been used.

This cartoon relies on the mother-in-law image alone as someone who has taken over the television set and her son-in-law's armchair.

"It's you who wants to watch snooker on the other side — you tell Mother!"

The strange thing about stereotypes is that they nearly always demonstrate negative values about individuals or situations. Very often, they stem from social and cultural values which show prejudice on our part.

The following worksheets are intended to help you to structure your ideas about stereotyping but, of course, stereotypes are not only found in comic situations.

Look at the two cartoons below:

" Remember you reversed the car into the garage last night? Well, I reversed it out this morning!"

" Well, did you go and make the last payment on the car?"

QUESTIONS	ANSWERS
Each cartoon shows two people — who are they?	
What is the thing the people are talking about in each cartoon?	
What has the woman in each cartoon done?	
Why do you think the cartoonist has made the woman do this and not the man?	
What is the stereotype in these cartoons?	

Look at the cartoon below:

"I think I've detected the problem —
Madam needs smaller feet!"

QUESTIONS	ANSWERS
Who is talking in the cartoon?	
Who is the man and what is he doing?	
Why is the woman looking so annoyed	
What STEREOTYPE image do you think the cartoonist has used?	
Do you think that this image is the truth?	

Summary of the main points raised in this chapter.

Three questions are asked about representations:

  (i)   Who makes representations?
 (ii)   How are representations made?
(iii)   Who are representations aimed at?

Representations are created across a range of media.

Because we look for "reality" in media constructs, we are likely to look for the "truth" in representations instead of treating them as media constructs.

Audiences negotiate meanings with media texts on the basis of their own social and cultural values in relation to those of society at large.

Audiences are likely, therefore, to accept media constructs, accept them with reservations, or to reject them outright.

Stereotypes are simplified generalisations about people or nations which are used extensively in the media to "get a message across" quickly. Stereotypes are often used in comedy programmes and cartoons, amongst other media forms. Often they concentrate on negative rather than the positive aspects of the people or nations concerned.

Notes;

1.   See John Fiske, *Introduction to Communication Studies*, Methuen (1982), pages 113/115.

CHAPTER SEVEN

TACKLING THE QUESTIONS

In this chapter you will find a selection of questions from past examination papers together with suggestions about how to tackle exam questions.

It is always useful to know what kind of questions you will be faced with during your exam and you should look carefully at the questions in this section.

Obviously, exam questions will be based on the areas which the Scottish Examination Board have specified. The questions, therefore, will explore the following prescribed areas: Film, Narrative and Representations.

Questions will be clearly worded, showing which area(s) the examiners wish the candidates to explore. Candidates, however, must be extremely careful about identifying exactly what the examiners want the candidates to analyse, discuss or illustrate within these given areas.

Take, for example, the question below, which appeared in Section D — Mass Media of the Specimen Question Paper, the Revised Arrangements for English, published by the Scottish Examination Board in 1987:

12. Write about a film you consider successful, describing what you believe to be its most important characteristics. Your account should distinguish between the contributions made to that success by at least four elements such as the use of stars, the direction, the script, acting, mise-en-scene, genre.

The question makes it immediately apparent that the candidate must discuss film: "Write about a film". This question, therefore, falls within the prescribed area of "Film".

Next, we can see a clear reference to the fact that you should write about a film which you think was "successful" and that the examiner expects you to write about the film's "most important characteristics". To ensure that there is no confusion about this matter, the examiner has given examples of what "important characteristics" means: "use of stars", "the direction", "the script", "acting", "mise-en-scene", "genre".

The candidate is told that the answer to this question should contain "at least four elements". Six elements have been listed, and so it is an easy matter to choose:

1. The film which you will base your answer on, and
2. The "characteristics" which made the film successful by referring to four of the six examples provided.

Now look at this selection of questions from Section D — Mass Media, Higher Grade Paper II, Writing, 1990:

11. Choose a film from a recognisable genre. To what extent did your enjoyment of the film depend on its conforming (or not) to the conventions of the genre?

12. How far do you agree with the charge that the commercial success of films set in Scotland has been bought at the expense of stereotyped representations of the Scots and their country? (You should refer to at least two films in your answer.)

14. "In order to attract the maximum audience during its particular time slots, soap opera must negotiate with that target audience, a large proportion of whom are female, working class, over fifty or under sixteen — social groups which are often otherwise regarded, in different degrees, as subordinate."
    To what extent does soap opera appear to you to be constructed for the audience described above? (You should refer to more than one soap opera in your answer.)

15. By referring to the same narrative related in two or more media, describe the extent to which a change of medium affected the narrative and your response to it.

These questions from the 1990 paper deal with the following: film genre, Scottish stereotypes in film, audience and narrative respectively.

In order to answer any of these questions, you should have a firm grasp of the underlying concept involved and several examples, drawn from your own experience of the media, which could be employed when structuring your answer, e.g. to answer question 11, you would require to know what is meant by film genre and have first hand knowledge of films which you have watched, either in part or from beginning to end, which you could discuss in your answer.

Tackling the exam question:

1. Identify from the question which aspects of the media the examiners wish you to discuss.

2. Read the question over again, carefully noting how the question is phrased.

3. Decide whether or not you know enough to answer the question. Sometimes, candidates do not read questions carefully enough and realise half way through their answer that they cannot satisfy the particular demands of that question.

4. If you are satisfied that you have enough information to formulate a full answer to the question, begin making rough notes of the ideas which immediately strike you, so that you do not have to rely solely on your memory whilst structuring your answer.

5. Include key phrases from the question throughout your answer. This serves two purposes:

    (i) The examiner will clearly see that you have noted the main points of the question and that you are attempting to answer these.

(ii) By including key phrases throughout, these will remind you about all the points you wish to make.

Now, look at the following example of how you might have structured an answer to question 11 of the 1990 paper:

> "Choose a film from a recognised genre. To what extent did your enjoyment of the film depend on its conforming (or not) to the conventions of the genre?"

Suggested plan:

(a) Title of the film you have chosen to discuss, with a clear reference to its genre; brief statement giving your point of view as to whether or not the film you are using in your answer conformed to the conventions of the genre.

Use wording from the question to link your paragraphs.

(b) Select reasons why the film met or did not meet conventions of genre. Bearing in mind that you must prove either way that you understand genre: Westerns, gangsters, musicals, science fiction, etc. Demonstrate your knowledge by analysing and discussing why your film does or does not meet the criterion of genre.

Use wording from the question to link your paragraphs.

(c) State how these points affected your enjoyment of the film. Base this on the information you have given in the paragraphs based on the suggestions for *(b)* above.

(d) Conclude by discussing genre in relation to your answer, so far.

An example of a possible finished answer to this question is shown on the following page.

A film which I thoroughly enjoyed watching was *Indiana Jones and the Temple of Doom*. I recognised that this film was an adventure film because there were many dangerous and exciting incidents in the film, usually involving the hero and heroine in narrow escapes from death. The film was set, like many adventure films, in "foreign" locations: in this case, China and India. Furthermore, in keeping with the classic adventure story, the hero wins in the end and good triumphs over evil.

My enjoyment of the film was enhanced because I liked the main character, Indiana Jones, who embodied all the classic ingredients of the "hero". He was strong, and handsome in a rugged way; he took control of the situation when things got out of hand; he was quick-thinking and very brave, overcoming all the obstacles in his path, which is quite satisfying in view of the fact that life is not always like this. Perhaps this is one of the main attractions of adventure films; the audience can escape from reality for a little while.

In contrast with Indiana's "hero" image, the heroine was typical of many: she was helpless, blonde and a bit stupid. In fact, she seemed to fall into the "dumb blonde" category of the female stereotype. I didn't enjoy this aspect of the film because I think that this kind of image of women, which is quite common in the media, is very derogatory, although it is a common enough image in adventure films if there are women characters.

The settings of the film were realistic, the action taking place, first of all, in China and then moving rapidly to India; both of which are considered rather mysterious and "foreign" places to people from the West, especially if — as is the case with this film — the narrative time is in the recent past. The mise-en-scene depicted these countries as we might imagine them in the 1930s, with overcrowded narrow streets in China, old cars, ancient aeroplanes and, in India, scenes showing the jungle, and elephants being used as transport, all of which made the settings quite exotic.

The episodic nature of the narrative — moving rapidly from incident to incident — can be clearly seen in the opening sequences of the film. The story begins in China, with Indiana Jones becoming involved in a brawl inside a crowded hotel dining room. Poison has been put in his drink. The ensuing brawl to lay claim to a glass phial with the antidote and a diamond rightfully belonging to Indiana, is depicted by a skillful montage of camera shots. The images cut swiftly from floor level to long shots of the crowded, chaotic room where the brawl takes place. This involves the audience in the frenetic activity of the fight and a gripping (and humorous) few moments occurs when shots of the glass phial, kicked around by trampling feet, are juxtaposed with shots of the diamond sliding around the floor as it, too, is accidentally kicked. Suspense is heightened because we think the phial might be trampled underfoot and the diamond lost. At last, Indiana finds the antidote and drinks it. He will live! This is typical of many of the adventurous, and humorous, incidents which happen throughout the narrative.

The film, therefore, was enjoyable because I liked Indiana Jones as the kind of classic hero figure usually found in adventure stories, the setting was exotic and helped to add to the escapism which I enjoy in films of this genre. I didn't like the image of the "dumb blonde" for the heroine, although I can understand why it is often a feature of these films: it is less trouble to have a stereotypical female figure. If she had been a strong personality who was as clever as Indiana Jones, this would have changed the story, entirely.

Indiana Jones and the Temple of Doom, therefore, is a classic example of the adventure film, conforming to this genre by virtue of the excitement and suspense in the story, the typical hero and heroine, the exotic setting and the satisfying ending, in which good (Indiana Jones) triumphs over evil (the wicked devil worshippers).

It should now be apparent that your answers should contain clear reference to *all* the points which the examiner asks about in the question: in this case how your enjoyment of a film depended on the usual ingredients which you would find in a certain kind of film.

Careful structuring of your answer is essential. The examiners will be looking for a clear, well-structured piece of continuous prose which is expected to be "substantial", about 500 words in length.

One further — very important point — should be borne in mind: you will be expected, prior to the commencement of your exam to write down, on the form which will be provided, the following information:

1.   Which main text(s) you used in your Review of Personal Reading.

2.   The texts used in Paper I (Reading) in the Specified Texts Section and those texts used for your Critical Essay.

The reason why you must do this is to ensure that you do not use any texts in Part 2 of your Writing paper which you have already used in your written response to Reading during the exam, or your Review of Personal Reading completed in the classroom. In other words, if you have used a script from radio, television or film as the subject of your Review of Personal Reading, you cannot use the same text again, to answer a Writing question.

Do your personal best. If your answer is an honest personal response to the question, shows a knowledge of basic critical terminology, and is technically of a good standard (i.e. correct punctuation, sentence construction, spelling, etc.), then you stand a very good chance of impressing the examiner.

Good luck!

CHAPTER EIGHT

SELECT ANNOTATED BIBLIOGRAPHY

The texts listed below have been coded according to their uses in the following way:

Useful for studying Film ☆
Useful for studying Narrative ◊
Useful for studying Representations +

If a text contains information which would be useful in more than one area, then you will see a combination of the codes, e.g. if a text is useful for both film and representations, it will be coded thus: ☆ + .

Some texts contain no code. This indicates that they are of general use rather than of specific use.

The author's names are listed with surnames first, then forenames, then the title of the text, the publisher, and the date of publication. Each text has been annotated, providing some guidance about contents and degree of usefulness.

Hopefully, your school, college, or local library service may be able to supply many of the titles listed.

Barrow, Eric. *Documentary, A History of the Non-fiction Film*, Oxford University Press (1974) ☆
    A very basic overview of documentary film.

Berger, J. and Mohr, J., *Another Way of Telling*, Writers and Readers, (1982) ◊
    Contains an essay about photographic communication and a photo-essay.

Bethell, A., *Eye Openers (One and Two)*, Cambridge University Press, (1981) ◊
> These two booklets are excellent introductions to the idea of "reading" photographs and visual narrative. They are, however, intended for classroom use but, nevertheless, students would gain much from individual study with these books. Book Two looks at news photographs and advertising images.

Butts, David (Ed.), *Advertising in Action; On Your Radio; Looking into Advertising; Planning the Schedules; Thinking about Images*, Hodder and Stoughton, (1987) ◊ +
> This is a series which is worth looking at. The books are presented in an interesting way and contain exercises for individuals and classroom work. They are simple to follow and, together, make a good introduction to the media.

Cook, Jim (Ed.), *Television Sitcom*, British Film Institute (1984) ◊ +
> See, in particular, page 13, "Narrative, Comedy, Characters and Performance" by Jim Cook and page 43, "The Gender Game" by Andy Medhurst and Lucy Tuck.

Cook, Pam (Ed.), *The Cinema Book*, British Film Institute (1987) ☆ ◊
> This is an excellent text which contains a wealth of information about film and film narrative.

Davis, Howard; Walton, Paul, *Language, Image, Media*, Basil Blackwell (1983) ◊
> See Chapter 11: "Seeing Sense" by Victor Burgin. Look at pages 234, 242/243 in this chapter for a discussion about images and narrative in photographs.

Dick, Eddie (Ed.), *From Limelight to Satellite*, Scottish Film Council/British Film Institute (1990) ☆
> This book contains a selection of essays looking at film, audiences and production circumstances. It also contains the first feature-film filmography of Scotland on Film from earliest times (1898 to date) with 300 titles.

73

Dutton, Brian, *The Media*, Longman (1986) +
Although this is a sociology text and not a media studies text, it contains a section on representations (Chapter 3) which provides a brief overview of some of the political and cultural arguments which surround representations and the media.

Dutton, Brian et al, *Media Studies: An Introduction*, Longman (1989) ☆ ◊ +
This is really a teaching text book with exercises for class work. You may, however, find it in the school library or elsewhere. The text contains a good general overview of all media but does not deal in depth with any specific media forms. The subjects covered are: the language for media studies, e.g. semiology, media institutions, representations, genre, audience and practical exercises for class work.

Film Education,
37–39 Oxford Street, London, W1R 1RE (071 434 9932) ☆ ◊
This is a useful address to know. Film Education produce teaching booklets intended for teachers to use, either for background knowledge of a subject or as material which can be used in the classroom. These booklets are distributed free of charge to schools. *Film: Genre* and *Film: Narrative; The Industry Pack: Production, Distribution, Exhibition* are useful booklets which provide information of a straight-forward nature. It is worth enquiring about other booklets which Film Education publish (especially booklets on individual films).

Fiske, John and Hartley, John, *Reading Television*, Methuen (1978) ◊
(Only for the most hardy readers.) Chapter Three: "The Signs of Television" is a useful introduction to the concepts of semiology. Chapter Six: "Bardic Television" is of most use in connection with ideologies and television as mediator. See, in particular, pages 85/89.

Fiske, John, *Introduction to Communication Studies*, Methuen (1982) ◊
See Chapter 6: "Semiotic Methods and Applications" (especially pages 107/110 for explanation about dominant, negotiated and oppositional decoding).

Fiske, John, *Television Culture*, Methuen (1987) ◊ +
A book which is worth dipping into although you will find some of it difficult. Contains a useful semiotic analysis of an extract from a television series, showing social, technical and ideological codes, pages 1–13. See pages 144 – 148 for a section on television narrative and references to television representations are scattered throughout but pages 149/151 compares television representations with those of the cinema.

Gunter, Barrie, *Television and Sex Role Stereotyping*, John Libbey & Company Ltd (1986) +
Contains research statistics relating to sex role stereotyping. Chapter Two is most useful.

Hardy, Forsyth, *Scotland in Film*, Edinburgh University Press (1990) ☆ +
Forsyth Hardy is a prominent figure in the Scottish film world and this book makes interesting reading.The book traces Scottish film making from its beginnings to the present and contains a useful up to date filmography of 150 Scottish films.

Hartley, John, *Understanding News*, Methuen (1982) ◊
Chapter Seven: "A Winter of Discontent" contains references to television news narrative. See in particular page 115 of that chapter for a comparison between television news narrative and television fictional narrative. This text can be a little difficult in places since it uses terminology connected with semiology but it is, nevertheless, a useful introduction to some of the ideas underlying semiological analysis of the news.

Hood, Stuart, *On Television*, Pluto Press (1980) +
Contains a section on television audiences which discusses the assumptions made about audiences.

Izod, John, *Reading the Screen: an introduction to film studies*, Longman York Press (1984) ☆
A short but useful introduction to film.

Izod, John, *Hollywood and the Box Office*, MacMillan (1987) ☆
This is a survey history of the American film industry. Shows how the film industry maximised profits through starring players, glamour, action and plots based on stories already familiar to the audience.

Monaco, James, *How to Read a Film*, Oxford University Press (1981) ☆
An excellent text to dip into, full of useful information about ideological and technical aspects of film making. Contains a good glossary of terms.

McArthur, Colin, *Scotch Reels*, BFI Publishing (1982) ☆ +
This text contains eight short essays (one of which is an interesting photographic essay) on the subject of Scotland on film and images of Scotland. Cairns Craig's essay, "Myths Against History: Tartanry and Kailyard in 19th Century Scottish Literature" traces the roots of the Romantic and Kailyard image of Scotland. Colin McArthur's essay "Scotland and Cinema: The Iniquity of the Fathers" is also useful in this connection.

McMahon, Barrie and Quin, Robyn, *Exploring Images*, Bookland, Western Australia (1984) +
Analysing and decoding images. A classroom text.

McMahon, Barrie and Quin, Robyn, *Real Images*, Macmillan (1986) ☆ ◊ +
Again, this is a classroom text book intended for teaching the media. You may be able to order it from your library. It contains useful information on film and television and is worth looking at.

McRoberts, Richard, *Media Workshop, Vols. 1 and 2: Words and Images*, McMillan (1987) ☆ +
Although these books have been produced for the Australian market, they are classroom text books which are useful introductions to the media.

Ontario Ministry for Education and Ontario Teachers' Education (which includes the Association for Media Literacy), *Media Literacy*. This A4 size book costs only $7 Canadian (about £3.50). Intended for Secondary School pupils, it is a useful reference book. It can be obtained at the following address:

Government of Ontario Book Store,
c/o Publications Department,
880 Bay Street,
5th Floor,
Toronto,
Ontario,
Canada M7A 1N8.

Root, Jane, *Open the Box*, Comedia (1986) +

This text about television is attractively presented and easy to read. It is not, however, organised into neat headings which would help students studying the mass media but Chapter 4: "People Who Tell You Things", is useful for those studying representations and there is a section on soap opera which is interesting.

CHAPTER NINE

GLOSSARY OF TERMS

A

Actor/actress: The role of actor or actress in the media does not differ in essence from that of actor or actress on the stage: in both cases the actor represents a character. In the media, however, the actor/actress works in a different environment from the stage setting and different demands are made upon their abilities. For example, by playing a part on the radio, the player requires to project character through voice, alone. On television and film, however, the actor or actress is seen in a variety of settings and, therefore, non-verbal signals (i.e. facial expression, gestures) become equally as important as voice and appearance. Furthermore, the media exposes the individual to a much larger audience than stage plays. There is more likelihood, therefore, of the actor or actress becoming "type-cast", i.e. becoming associated with one particular character in a part they have played in a film or television series.

Anchor/anchorage: To fix the meaning of images using words/the words which fix the meaning of a picture. Pictures can be interpreted in a number of ways, depending upon who is looking at them. The best way to fix the meaning of a picture is to add words to the picture.

Audience: Audience, for the purposes of media studies, is the vast number of anonymous people who "consume" the products of the mass media. This potentially includes the whole of society. As individuals, we help to make up audiences for a variety of different media. The media industries, however, often require to find out more about audiences in order that their products (for example, magazines, newspapers, television programmes, etc.) can be directed at a specific audience. Audiences, therefore, are often broken down into *age*, *gender* and *class* to make audience analyses easier.

Audience: age, gender and ***class:*** Audiences can generally be categorised under the headings of age, gender and class. This means that the demands of specific audiences can be taken into account when producing the media. The advertising industries, for example, are particularly anxious to attract the public to buy the products which their clients are selling. There would be no sense in scheduling a television advertisement for shaving cream on children's television, or advertising children's sweets late at night when presumably children will be in bed.

Audience: effect(s): Much research has been carried out to find out what effects the media have on audiences. It used to be thought that the media had a direct effect on individuals. For example, it was thought that if people were exposed to violent films, they themselves would become violent. This was called the "hypodermic" theory, i.e. the public were being metaphorically "injected" with the media. Subsequent research has shown that it is not so simple as this and that the individuals who comprise a media audience are not only influenced by the media but by their own upbringing and their place in society. The question of media effects, however, remains a complicated one, influenced by many different points of view.

Audience: expectations: The preconceived ideas which an audience harbours about what kind of experience they are going to have from viewing, reading, or listening to the media.

Audience: image: It could be said that the media "create" their audiences, i.e. the media tailor output to what they think an audience will want. In order to do this successfully, the media industries must have an "image" of their audience(s).

Authorship (auteur): This usually refers to a director who produces his/her films in such a way that they are always immediately recognisable as being his/hers.

B

Broadcast(ing) (see also '**narrowcast**'): Used in connection with television and radio. In theory, anyone who has a receiver (i.e. a television or a radio) and who is close enough to the transmitters, can receive the messages sent by television and radio stations. The audiences for television and radio programmes are, therefore, mass audiences, i.e. millions of people can receive the programmes.

C

Camera angle(s): The angle at which a camera points at a subject changes the audience's point of view. For example, if the camera is placed high above the subject, this can have various effects such as making the subject look smaller, less significant, or allows the audience to see what the subject is doing in greater detail. If the camera is placed low and is pointing up towards the subject, this might make the subject look taller and more threatening.

Camera technician: Used in this book to describe someone who is trained to operate a camera.

Channels: Television and radio transmitters operate on certain frequencies which have been set aside for them. Our television and radios are tuned to receive signals on these frequencies. When we communicate, we are said to be using channels of communication, e.g. voice, sight, etc.

Classic Narrative: (See **Narrative**).

Code: Used in connection with communication, a system of *signs* which are controlled by rules followed by members of a society. Codes help us to organise information. They should never be seen as a set of rules applied like algebraic formula but as an integral part of communication. People in society use these codes quite naturally, without thinking about them.

Codes: dominant: Codes which convey strong messages about the dominant values of society.

Codes: oppositional: The rejection of dominant values. Although the person recognises and understands the dominant values in a message, she/he prefers to oppose these.

Codes: negotiated: Acceptance of the dominant values but able to see that there is room for argument or negotiation.

Communication: There is no single definition of communication. Theorists, however, work on the principle that there are two different kinds of communication. One, broadly speaking, occurs when a signal is sent from A to B. It is assumed that this signal will affect B in some way. This definition can be used to speak about both mechanical and human communication. For example, an electrical impulse (signal) can be sent through a cable to an explosive device which explodes when the impulse reaches it. Similarly your friend can send a signal (speak to you) by vibrating his vocal chords which, in turn causes a signal to be received in your brain. You will react in some way to this signal — even if it is only to ignore what you hear! The other kind of communication is said to consist of an exchange of meaning in which both sender and receiver are creating meaning. For example, your friend chooses words, phrases, and tone of voice to get the message across to you, thereby, creating meaning. You, in turn, are making your own meanings from the combination of sounds, gestures and expressions which your friend is using.

Connotations: The layers of social meaning which surround something. For example, the colour white means purity in this society (think of the bridal gown) whereas in other societies white is the colour of mourning.

Construct(ed): This word relates to the ideas contained in the second kind of communication mentioned above (see **Communication**). Meaning could be said to be constructed by, for example, a photographer taking a photograph. He will decide to use a certain camera angle, lighting, shutter speed, etc., to show his subject in a particular way and in doing so "constructs" the meaning of the picture. When the picture is viewed by others, they will also "construct" meanings of their own by looking at what is in the picture. Something put together in this way is said to be a construct.

Convention(s): The habits of thinking shared by members of a particular culture.

Credits: The list of actors and actresses, technicians and others who have helped to make a film

Cultural knowledge: A framework of knowledge shared by those in the same culture which encourages certain ways of interpreting information.

D

Decoding: The act of making meaning from codes.

Diegesis: Everything which you see and hear during a film which helps the narrative along. The diegesic effect of a film is gained through viewing and listening. Through the viewer's observations, the idea of space and time is conveyed as well as deeper meanings associated with social and cultural ideas.

Direct(or)(ing): The person who controls the actors, camera operators and other crew when making a film, television or radio programme.

Dominant (readings) (see **Codes: dominant**).

E

Edit(or)(ing): Editing involves making, or suggesting that, alterations should be made to books, magazines, newspapers, films, etc. An **Editor** carries out these functions. e.g. A newspaper editor is likely to cut stories down to size. A film editor will cut film and splice it together again into the final form the film will take.

Enigma: *(or narrative "hook"):* Something puzzling in a story which makes the viewer/reader want to continue viewing/reading in order to find out an answer.

F

Fade: Used in film or television, the fade breaks a story up into separate parts. During a **fade in** the screen is black to begin with and then it brightens until we can see a picture. During a **fade out** the opposite happens; the image on the screen will gradually fade away until there is a black screen.

Feedback: Used in communication, feedback means that the reaction of the person receiving information is "fed back" or transmitted back to the person sending the message, e.g. if you are angry with someone, you might raise your voice sharply. This might make the person flinch. If you see this and know that it happened as a result of your raised voice, you will have had feedback from your communication.

Feedback is also used to describe what happens when electronic systems which have "input" and "output" return some of their "output" to the "input". e.g. If microphones are placed too near loud-speaker systems, they will make a loud howling sound because the "output" system (the loud-speaker) is causing a feedback to the "input" system (the microphones).

Film: The celluloid strip coated with light-sensitive material which, when exposed to an image by a camera, will, after chemical treatment, produce a negative of that image. A sequence of such images on a film strip.

Frame: An image from a sequence of images on a film strip.

G

Genre(s): Different media forms, e.g. in film, there is the science fiction genre, the Western genre, or in television there are the genres of drama, documentary, etc. Genre is also used to describe books and means the same thing, i.e. different kinds, or categories, of books; romance, thriller, etc.

H

Headline: The title given to a news article in a newspaper and printed in large bold type at the top of the article. The news summary given at the beginning of a television or radio broadcast.

"High-Key" (See **Key lighting** and **Lighting**.)

"Hook" (narrative): (See **Enigma**.)

I

Image(s): An image is something which we see, e.g. a photograph. There are, however, other uses for the word which are based on *ideas*, e.g. a picture experienced mentally. Poets can create "images" by employing literary devices such as simile, metaphor, personification, which help the reader to "see" what the poet is describing. Pop stars can also create "images" by the kind of music which they play and by their appearance; clothing, hair styles, etc.

K

Key lighting: Lighting can be high- or low-key and the key lighting is the type of lighting which is used for most of a film scene, e.g. mostly dark lighting would be "low-key". (See under **Lighting**.)

L

Lighting: high-key: bright lighting used in a film scene. (See **Key lighting**.)

Lighting: low-key: dark lighting used in a film scene. (See **Key lighting**.)

Live (broadcast): A television or radio broadcast which is made at the time of an incident, i.e. the viewers/listeners are experiencing what is happening immediately it happens. e.g. a news item being relayed by satellite direct to our homes.

Low-key: (See under **Key lighting** and **Lighting**.)

M

Mass media: Media which are intended to reach vast audiences.

Medium: The method of communication, e.g. television is a medium of communication.

Message(s): Information conveyed or meaning negotiated by communicating.

Mise-en-scene: Camera movements, camera positioning, scenery, lighting, etc., in film.

Monochrome: One colour, e.g. of black and white films.

Montage: The process of editing film together. The study of how images have been juxtaposed to produce an effect.

N

Narrative: The structure or plot of a story. How the story is told.

Narrative: classic narrative: The most common narrative form in any medium. The story begins with a state of equilibrium which moves to disruption and back to equilibrium. When used of film, classic narrative means that the film is structured in such a way that there is clear movement from beginning to end of story, that the links in the story are clearly shown and that the story takes place in a credible fictional world, i.e. one in which the viewer can believe.

Narrative hook: (See **Enigma**.)

Narrowcast: The opposite of broadcasting (see **broadcast**). Narrowcasting occurs when messages are sent to a restricted audience, e.g. Citizens Band radio.

Negotiated (reading): (See **Codes: negotiated.**)

O

Oppositional (reading): (See **Code: oppositional.**)

P

Produce(r)(ing): The producer assumes overall responsibility for the making of a film or programme, taking into account money available, etc. The act of making a film or programme.

R

Receiver: The person or machine which receives a message.

Representation(s): Abstract ideas about people or groups of people in society as used by the media. These abstract notions are put into concrete form when we view, for example, a play on television depicting "the housewife" as female, devoted to "keeping house" for her family (usually her husband and two children) to the exclusion of everything else in life.

Satellite dish: A receiver used to pick up signals from satellites circulating the earth and which are used to transmit programmes from television stations around the world.

Satellite television: The name given to the programmes received from satellite communication, using satellite dishes.

Screenplay: The script for a film. This will include dialogue and stage directions.

Script(ing): The printed text of a programme to be screened on film or television, or radio. The act of writing such a text.

Semiologists: Those who make a study of **signs**.

Semiology: The study of **signs** as espoused by the French linguist, Saussure and the French philosopher, Roland Barthes. (See also **Semiotics**.)

Semiotics: The study of **signs** as espoused by the American philosopher, Charles Pierce. (See also **Semiology**.)

Sender: The person or machine which sends a message.

Senses: perception: The physiological aids to perception such as sight, hearing, touch, smell and taste.

Shots: The separate pieces of film (the length is immaterial) which are used to make up a cinema production. There may be hundreds or thousands of separate shots, or only one.

Signs: Units of meaning used in connection with **semiology** or **semiotics**.

Social and cultural knowledge: (See *Cultural Knowledge*.)

Sound technician: A specialist in sound.

Soundtrack: The mix of dialogue, sound effects and music on a piece of film or video.

Space: The illusion of space produced on film or video. (See *Diegesis*.)

Star: An actor or actress who has become famous in the film world and whose name is used as an attraction when marketing films.

Stereotypes: The generalisation of people and groups into simplified forms which rely on certain assumptions about their behaviour and characteristics.

Stereotypical: Behaviour, etc., which is seen to belong to ideas engendered by generalisations and assumptions about people or groups of people in society.

Syntagm: A combination of **signs**, making a whole, e.g. a sentence is a syntagm because each word has been chosen from a range of other words and put together to make a whole statement.

T

Technical codes: The codes employed within specific media industries, e.g. camera angle, lighting, etc., in the film and television industries.

Technicians: A word used in this book to indicate trained professionals who handle the technical side of media production.

Text: The medium or a part of the medium being studied, e.g. film, T.V. play, etc., or any part thereof.

The media: The collective term given to those industries which communicate to a mass audience, e.g. press, television, radio, cinema, etc.

Time: The illusion of the passage of time in a film.

Time Slot: The scheduling of a programme to be shown at a particular viewing or listening time.

APPENDIX I

(a)

Daily Record

22p FORWARD WITH SCOTLAND

No. 30,976

FIREWORK TERROR AT FESTIVAL!

■ FUN turned to terror at Glasgow's Garden Festival last night as crowds at the fireworks finale were blitzed

■ IT happened as 100,000 people watched what was to have been the spectacular end to a five-month

Sprint king Ben loses title

From ALEX CAMERON in Seoul

SPRINT king Ben Johnson was sensationally stripped of his Olympic title early today.

The Canadian 100 metres gold medallist now faces a LIFE ban from athletics after

b)

THE GLASGOW HERALD

CITY EDITION

SCOTLAND'S NEWSPAPER

206th year—No. 210

TUESDAY, SEPTEMBER 27, 1988

Johnson stripped of gold after failing drugs test

From DOUG GILLON

SEOUL, Tuesday

BEN JOHNSON, the newly crowned Olympic 100 metres champion, has been stripped of his gold medal after testing positive for body-building anabolic steroids.

Olympic spokeswoman Michelle Verdier said his urine sample contained the banned substance Stanoziol. He has been banned from the Games, and his world record of 9.79 seconds which he set on Saturday will not be ratified.

The International Commission of the International Olympic Committee had recommended the move to the IOC executive after the positive test.

The executive considered Canadian claims that the substance had been administered by a third party, but dismissed them. John-

son now faces a life ban from the sport by his government.

The findings will also be a financial blow for Johnson. Lyle McCoskey, Canada's assistant deputy minister of sport, said: "If any athlete is confirmed positive using any banned substance there will be an immediate withdrawal of financial support for life."

Johnson currently gets $1000 per month from the Federal government which will now cut it off in addition to his Olympic gold. He drives a $150,000 Ferrari and is reputedly negotiating for a $1.5m house near Ottawa. His agent, Larry Heidebrecht, last year negotiated a contract with the Italian sports goods company, Diadora, for a fee of $2.5m.

Heidebrecht reacted to the news with disbelief. "The only thing we can say at this stage is that it is a tragedy, a mistake or a

sabotage. Up to five days before the Games I was in perfect condition. Something has happened in those days.

"We do not know what happened and how it happened, but apparently somebody has sabotaged Ben and we will find out who it was and how it was done."

Johnson, who is staying at the Hilton Hotel here, was not in his room when I called this morning. Karen Astaphan, the wife of Johnson's doctor who is staying with the Canadian party, said Johnson was outraged by the comment and that his manager Charlie Francis had left the hotel.

This is the biggest drugs scandal at an Olympics since four years ago the Finn, Martti Vainio, was stripped of his Olympic silver medal in the 10,000 metres after he too had tested positive for the performance-enhancing steroids.

He had drawn off blood in order to boost the oxygen supply in his own system. The procedure involves retransfusing the blood after the body has made good the deficit. Some athletes use the blood he had been taking steroids, but he forgot about this and, although his system would otherwise have been cleared, the reintroduced blood was contaminated.

Already two Bulgarian gold medallists have been stripped of their titles as a result, including Angel Grabler, who set a world record. The remaining four members of the Bulgarian weightlifting team have returned home. Another Canadian weightlifter, Australian modern pentathlete Alexander Watson has been sent home after testing positive for excessive caffeine.

But just how Olympus has been shaken to its core by the

Johnson scandal can be gauged from the fact that the chairman of the commission, Prince Alexandre de Merode, of Belgium, was expected away from his bed after 4am in the Hilton Hotel and was so incensed at his sleep being disturbed that he demanded the switchboard block all other calls.

If Johnson is stripped of his title the crown will go to American Carl Lewis. Britain's Linford Christie would then move from bronze to silver.

Carl Lewis who was outspoken last year regarding drug abuse at the World Championships beat him in the final then some medal winners had used steroids.

It was in Rome that Johnson beat him for the world title, setting the previous world mark of 9.83 seconds which sadly now must also be tainted.

.......**Sports Opinion.......Back Page**

BEN JOHNSON: A test for body-building anabolic steroids proved positive after his defeat of Carl Lewis in 100 metres in the astounding time of 9.79 seconds.

First for Scotland

THE HERALD

IRISH ANGER OVER FREED SOLDIER

THE Irish Government last night expressed "surprise and deep concern" after a manslaughter charge against a teenage British soldier was dropped and said it would be "pursuing the matter". The charge against Private David Holden, 18, accused of killing an unarmed Roman Catholic at an Ulster border checkpoint was withdrawn when he appeared at Belfast

---

Explosion injures six at festival fireworks

By ELIZABETH BUIE, CONNIE HENDERSON and DAVID STEELE

SIX people were injured, three seriously, in last night's Glasgow Garden Festival farewell fireworks display when a firework

the Suffolk-based fireworks display company Shell-Shock. He founded the company in 1985 with two friends, all former em-

PICTURE: EDWARD JONES

NOTES

NOTES

NOTES

NOTES

ACKNOWLEDGEMENTS

The author and publisher are grateful to the following for permission to use copyright material in this book.

The cartoons from *The Weekly News*
are reproduced by kind permission of D.C. Thomson & Co. Ltd.,

The front page headline from the *Daily Record*
is reproduced by kind permission of the Scottish Daily Record.

The front page headline from the *Glasgow Herald*
is reproduced by courtesy of the Glasgow Herald.